WHAT IS DIGITAL MARKETING IN 2023?

Reinvent your marketing strategy with the latest trends and technologies

WHAT IS DIGITAL MARKETING IN 2024?

Reinvent your marketing strategy with the latest trends and technologies

Vincent Lefebvre

Ron Goldsmith
EDITIONS

ISBN-13: 9798871731116

Cover design by: Vincent Lefebvre

A mon fils Auguste

CONTENTS

PREFACE

By Jean Darmanin, Expert in Digital Marketing and Technological Innovation

In a world where change is the only constant, digital marketing continues to evolve at a dizzying pace, shaped by technological advances and societal transformations. As an expert in this dynamic field, I have had the privilege of witnessing and participating in these developments, observing how they are redefining the way brands engage with their audiences.

The book you hold in your hands is an in-depth and insightful exploration of this ever-changing landscape. Vincent Lefebvre, with remarkable expertise and foresight, guides us through the key digital marketing trends of 2024, unveiling the strategies, tools and techniques that are shaping the future of this industry.

From predictive analytics to artificial intelligence, augmented reality and blockchain, this book doesn't just describe the technologies; it explores their practical impact on marketing and how they can be used to create richer, more personalized customer experiences. Vincent Lefebvre not only offers us a vision of what digital marketing will be like in the near future, but also practical advice and case studies to illustrate how these concepts come to life in the real world.

This book is essential reading for marketing professionals, entrepreneurs, students, and anyone interested in the fascinating intersection between technology and marketing. As a reader, you will be equipped not only to understand current trends, but also to anticipate future changes, positioning you at the forefront of innovation in digital marketing.

Prepare to dive into a journey through the evolving digital marketing landscape, where innovation, creativity and strategy meet to shape the future of how we connect, communicate and convert in the digital world .

INTRODUCTION

"The biggest risk is to take no risks."
Mark Zuckerberg

1.1. Definition and Scope

Imagine a world where every interaction, every click, every share on the Internet shapes a story, a story that speaks about you, about me, about all of us. This is where digital marketing comes to life. But what is digital marketing really in 2024? It's not just about ads or social media posts. It is a complex web, woven with finesse, connecting technologies, strategies, and human stories.

Digital marketing, at its essence, is this ongoing conversation between brands and consumers, facilitated through a myriad of digital channels. It encompasses everything from SEO, which helps people find the answers to their questions on Google, to Facebook ads that seem to know your needs before you even do. In 2024, this definition has expanded, embracing advanced technologies like artificial intelligence, augmented reality, and more.

But why is it important to you? Because, whether you are an entrepreneur, a student, an artist, or simply curious about digital technology, understanding digital marketing is like holding the key to an immense and constantly evolving kingdom. It's understanding how messages are targeted, how brands connect with their audiences, and how, ultimately, these interactions shape our society.

In this journey through digital marketing in 2024, you will discover not only its components, but also its impact and scope. You'll see how it influences purchasing decisions, shapes opinions, and builds communities. And most importantly, you will learn how it can be used ethically and effectively to create a better, more connected and more conscious world.

So, embark on this adventure. Discover how digital marketing has evolved, how it works now, and above all, how it will shape our future.

1.2. Historical Development

To fully appreciate the digital marketing landscape in 2024, it is essential to take a look back, to understand where we came from. Digital marketing, as we know it today, is the result of a fascinating evolution, a dance between technology and human needs, between innovation and creativity.

Let's go back to the 1990s, the dawn of the digital age. It was the time when the Internet was making its first steps into homes. Websites were simple, often just text on a plain background. Digital marketing at that time was rudimentary – think of banner ads, the first marketing emails. It was new, exciting, but still very basic.

Then came the new millennium, and with it, a revolution. Search engines like Google have started to shape the web. SEO was born, transforming the way content is found and consumed. Businesses began to understand the importance of being visible online, and digital marketing took on a new dimension.

The 2010s marked the meteoric rise of social networks. Facebook, Twitter, Instagram, and later TikTok, have redefined communication. Digital marketing has become more personal, more direct. Brands no longer spoke "to" their audience, but "with" them. It was the era of engagement, of content creation, of storytelling.

And now, in 2024, we are in the age of hyper-personalization and technological integration. Artificial intelligence and data science have transformed digital marketing into a tailor-made experience. Every online interaction is analyzed, every data is used to create more relevant, more effective campaigns. Augmented reality and virtual reality have opened new frontiers, enabling immersive and interactive experiences.

This development is not just technological. It

reflects a change in our way of communicating, consuming and living. Digital marketing in 2024 is not just a set of tools and techniques. It is a mirror of our society, of our values, of our aspirations.

By understanding this story, you'll never see a simple online ad the same way again. You will see a chapter of an ever-changing story, a story where you are both spectator and actor.

1.3. Importance in the Modern World

In the fast-paced world of 2024, digital marketing is not just a facet of commerce or communication, it is a central pillar of our modern society. Its importance transcends simple advertising or product promotion. It shapes our culture, influences our choices, and is a key driver of innovation and economic growth.

First, let's consider the impact of digital marketing on the economy. Businesses, from startups to multinationals, depend on digital marketing to reach their customers. In a world where the majority of consumers spend a large part of their time online, being visible on the web is not a luxury, but a necessity. Digital marketing allows businesses to connect with their audiences in a targeted and measurable way, often delivering a much higher return on investment than traditional methods.

But the importance of digital marketing goes well beyond turnover. It plays a crucial role in the construction and dissemination of ideas and values. Online awareness campaigns, for example, have the power to mobilize millions of people around social and environmental causes. Social networks, blogs, videos – all these tools allow us to share stories, spark debate, create communities. Digital marketing has become a vector of social change.

Additionally, digital marketing is fertile ground for innovation. Advances in artificial intelligence, data analytics, augmented and virtual reality – all find practical and powerful applications in digital marketing. These technologies don't just make marketing more effective; they are transforming the way we interact with the digital world, enriching our online experience in ways unimaginable a few years ago.

Finally, digital marketing is essential for education and information. In a world where information is abundant, digital marketing helps filter, organize and present this information in an accessible way. Whether through video tutorials, educational blogs, or interactive webinars, digital marketing is a powerful tool for sharing knowledge and encouraging lifelong learning.

In short, digital marketing in 2024 is much more than a series of business strategies. It is an integral part of our daily lives, influencing the way we think, interact, and evolve as a society. To understand its importance is to understand a crucial aspect of our times.

CHAPTER 1: THE FUNDAMENTALS OF DIGITAL MARKETING

"The best way to predict the future is to create it."
Peter Drucker

1.1 SEO: Search Engine Optimization

1.1.1 SEO Basics

Search engine optimization, or SEO, is a subtle art, a science that is constantly evolving. At the heart of this discipline is a simple but powerful goal: improving the visibility and relevance of a website in search results. But how exactly do we get there in 2024? Let's start with the basics.

SEO is based on three fundamental pillars: technique, content, and authority. The technical part concerns the optimization of the structure of the website. This includes page loading speed, mobile friendliness, and clear site architecture. A well-structured site is like a well-organized library, where every book is easy to find.

Next, the content. It's not just about quantity, but quality and relevance. Search engines, with their sophisticated algorithms, seek to understand the content of a site as a human would. They analyze the words, the context, the freshness of the content. Good content not only answers users' questions but also provides them with an enriching experience.

Finally, authority. This often comes down to links from other websites. Think of these links as recommendations. The more a site is recommended by trusted sources, the more it is considered an authority in its field. However, in 2024, link quality takes precedence over quantity. One link from a reputable site is worth much more than hundreds of low-quality links.

But SEO doesn't stop there. It is an ever-evolving discipline, shaped by changes in user behaviors and updates to search engine algorithms. Today, things like user experience (UX), search intent, and even artificial intelligence play a crucial role in a site's SEO.

By understanding these basic principles, you have taken the first step towards mastering SEO.

It's a fascinating journey, where every small improvement can lead to significant results. In the following sections, we'll explore each of these pillars in detail, providing you with the knowledge and tools needed to excel in the dynamic world of SEO.

1.1.2 Technical and On-Page SEO

Technical and on-page SEO are the foundations on which the entire building of natural referencing rests. In 2024, these aspects of SEO have increased in complexity, but understanding them remains essential for anyone who wants to successfully navigate the world of digital marketing.

Technical SEO focuses on optimizing the structure of the website. It starts with page loading speed. In a world where every second counts, a fast site is a site that retains its visitors. Search engines favor sites that load quickly, providing a better user experience. This involves optimizing images, using caching, and sometimes minifying JavaScript code.

Then there's mobile friendliness. With the prevalence of smartphones, a site that is not optimized for mobile devices is a site that is missing out on a significant portion of its audience. Responsive design is not an option, it's a necessity. Search engines, especially Google, favor mobile-friendly sites in their rankings.

Site architecture also plays a crucial role. A

clear and logical structure not only helps users navigate the site, but also allows search engines to better understand and index the content. This includes using appropriate HTML tags, creating an XML sitemap, and establishing a consistent URL structure.

Now let's move on to on-page SEO. Here, the focus is on optimizing the content of each page. It starts with title tags and meta descriptions. These elements, although often overlooked, are essential. They act as a storefront for each page, giving users and search engines a quick overview of the page's content.

The content itself should be high quality, relevant and provide value to readers. In 2024, search engines have become incredibly good at evaluating content quality. They are looking for original, well-written information that directly responds to users' search intentions. The use of keywords is still important, but it must be natural and contextual.

Finally, image optimization is another crucial aspect of on-page SEO. Images should be high quality, but also optimized for the web. This means reduced file sizes without sacrificing clarity, and the use of alt tags to describe image content, which is essential for SEO and accessibility.

By mastering technical and on-page SEO, you put in place the solid foundations necessary for a successful website. It's an investment that pays off, not only in terms of search engine rankings, but also in providing a great user experience.

1.1.3 Off-Page SEO and Backlinks

Off-page SEO and backlinks are the external pillars of SEO, playing a crucial role in how a website is perceived and evaluated by search engines. In 2024, these aspects of SEO have evolved, but their fundamental importance remains unchanged. They represent the reputation and credibility of a site in the vast universe of the Internet.

Off-page SEO primarily focuses on backlinks, which are inbound links to your site from other domains. These links are like votes of confidence in the eyes of search engines. The more quality links a site receives from reputable sites, the more it is considered a reliable and authoritative source. However, the key lies in quality, not quantity. A single link from a high-authority website can be much more valuable than dozens of links from lower-quality sites.

In 2024, the way these backlinks are obtained has also evolved. Artificial or manipulative link building practices are not only ineffective, but can also damage a site's reputation. Effective off-page SEO strategies often involve creating quality content that naturally attracts backlinks, participating in online communities, and collaborating with other websites and influencers in your niche.

Another important aspect of off-page SEO is

the presence on social networks. Although links from these platforms are not typically considered backlinks in the traditional sense, they play a significant role in building brand awareness and authority. An active and engaging social media presence can not only attract traffic to your site, but also encourage shares and mentions, which are positive signals for search engines.

Additionally, brand mentions, even without a link, have become an important factor in off-page SEO. Search engines, thanks to sophisticated algorithms, are able to recognize and evaluate these mentions. They contribute to the overall authority of a site, even if they are not accompanied by a hyperlink.

Finally, it is essential to monitor and manage online reputation. Reviews and comments on third-party sites, forums, and review platforms can influence the perception of your brand and, by extension, your SEO performance. Proactive online reputation management, including responding to reviews and participating in relevant discussions, is a key part of off-page SEO.

In summary, off-page SEO and backlinks in 2024 are not just about accumulating links, but about building a solid and respected online presence. This involves a holistic strategy that encompasses quality content creation, social media engagement, online reputation management, and building authentic relationships across the digital ecosystem.

1.1.4 Local and Mobile SEO

In the vast world of SEO, two aspects particularly stand out in 2024: local SEO and mobile SEO. These two facets of natural referencing meet specific needs and reflect current trends in consumption and Internet use.

Local SEO has become essential for businesses and brands that operate locally or have physical points of sale. It's the art of optimizing your online presence to attract customers from your area or city. In a world where "near me" or "near me" searches are commonplace, ranking well in local search results is crucial. This involves optimizing your Google My Business listing, collecting local reviews, and using location-based keywords in your content. Good local SEO helps your business stand out in the local community, attract more customers to your store or generate phone calls.

On the other hand, mobile SEO takes into account user experience on mobile devices. With the steady increase in the use of smartphones to access the Internet, search engines, especially Google, have started favoring mobile-optimized sites. This means that your site should not only be responsive, adapting to different screen sizes, but also provide a smooth and fast user experience on mobile. Mobile optimization includes things like fast loading times, easily clickable buttons and links, and a design that makes it easy to navigate on a small screen. In 2024, a site that is not optimized for mobile risks losing a significant part of its traffic and visibility.

Local and mobile SEO are closely related because many local searches are performed on mobile devices. Users search for information on the go, often with the intention of taking immediate action, whether to find a restaurant, store, or service. Thus, an effective SEO strategy in 2024 must integrate these two aspects to meet the needs of local and mobile users.

In summary, local and mobile SEO are essential components of an overall SEO strategy in 2024. They address specific search behaviors and are crucial for businesses looking to attract a local customer base and provide an optimal user experience on mobile devices. By integrating them into your SEO strategy, you ensure you don't miss valuable opportunities in an increasingly mobile and localized world.

1.2 Online Advertising

1.2.1. Overview of advertising platforms

In the dynamic field of online advertising in 2024, the panorama of advertising platforms is as diverse as it is innovative. These platforms offer a wide range of options for targeting, engaging and converting varied audiences, each with their own specificities and benefits.

Traditional giants like Google and Facebook continue to dominate the market, offering sophisticated targeting capabilities based on demographics, interests, and purchasing behaviors. Google, with its Search Network and Display Platform, allows advertisers to position themselves precisely where users are actively searching for information. Facebook, on the other hand, excels at creating highly personalized campaigns thanks to its in-depth knowledge of its users' preferences and habits.

At the same time, platforms like Instagram, Snapchat, and TikTok attract a younger and more engaged audience. These social networks, focused on visuals and video, offer unique opportunities for creative and immersive campaigns. TikTok, in particular, has revolutionized online advertising with its short and captivating formats, becoming a privileged playground for brands targeting a young and trendy audience.

LinkedIn continues to be the platform of choice for B2B marketing, providing direct access to key professionals and decision-makers across various industries. Its ability to target based on specific professional criteria, such as industry, company size, or position, makes it an invaluable tool for B2B campaigns.

Additionally, the emergence of programmatic advertising has transformed the way advertising space is bought and sold. Thanks to automation and artificial intelligence, advertisers can now buy advertising space in real time, targeting specific audiences across a multitude of websites and apps, maximizing the effectiveness and ROI of their campaigns .

Finally, it is important to note the rise of streaming platforms like Spotify and Netflix, which have opened new avenues for audio and video advertising. These platforms offer unique advertising experiences, often seamlessly integrated into content, which can increase audience engagement and receptivity.

Overall, the advertising platform landscape in 2024 is a rich and diverse ecosystem, providing advertisers with a multitude of options to reach their target audiences. The key to success lies in understanding the strengths of each platform and integrating these tools into a cohesive, well-targeted advertising strategy.

1.2.2. Search engine advertising

Search engine advertising, a core element of digital marketing in 2024, continues to play a crucial role in the strategy of any business seeking to increase its online visibility. This form of advertising, often dominated by Google Ads, has become more sophisticated and integrated, reflecting technological advances and changes in user behavior.

At the heart of search engine advertising is the

concept of "pay-per-click" (PPC), where advertisers pay for each click on their ads. This model is extremely effective because it allows you to target users who are actively looking for specific products or services. In 2024, targeting capabilities have become more precise, allowing advertisers to target audiences based on criteria such as location, interests, search habits, and even purchasing behaviors.

Google Ads, the most popular platform for search engine advertising, offers a variety of ad formats, including traditional text ads, display ads, and video ads. These ads appear not only in Google search results, but also on other partner websites in the Google Display Network. This diversity of formats allows advertisers to choose the best way to communicate their message and engage their target audience.

Optimizing search engine advertising campaigns has become more complex and more data-driven. Advertisers use advanced analytics and tracking tools to measure the performance of their campaigns, adjust their bids in real time, and optimize their keywords and advertising messages. Artificial intelligence plays a growing role in this optimization, helping to predict user behaviors and automate campaign adjustments to maximize ROI.

Additionally, search engine advertising in 2024 is no longer just about direct sales. It is also used to build brand awareness, educate consumers, and even influence purchasing decisions early in the customer journey. Advertisers often combine search engine advertising with other forms of digital marketing, such as SEO and content marketing, to create a comprehensive and cohesive online marketing strategy.

In conclusion, search engine advertising in 2024 is a powerful and indispensable tool for businesses of all sizes. It offers immediate visibility, precise targeting, and high conversion opportunities, while integrating seamlessly into a broader digital marketing strategy. For businesses looking to stand out in a crowded marketplace, mastering search engine advertising is not only beneficial, but essential.

1.2.3. Social media advertising

Advertising on social networks, in 2024, has become an essential element of any digital marketing strategy. With social platforms constantly evolving and increasing their influence, brands have a powerful tool at their disposal to reach and engage their target audience in a direct and personal way.

Each social network offers its own particularities and advantages in terms of advertising. Facebook, for example, remains a platform of choice for targeting a large and diverse audience, thanks to its detailed targeting options that include demographic, behavioral, and even psychographic criteria. Instagram, with its emphasis on visuals, is ideal for brands looking to create aesthetically appealing and engaging ad campaigns that are particularly effective at reaching younger audiences.

TikTok, which has become a social media giant, offers a unique platform for creative and viral campaigns, especially among Generation Z. Its dynamic and short-form video content-oriented nature makes it a fertile ground for innovative and captivating advertising campaigns . LinkedIn, meanwhile, continues to dominate the B2B advertising industry, providing direct access to professionals and decision-makers across various industries.

One of the most appealing aspects of social media advertising is its ability to engage directly with consumers. Brands can not only broadcast their messages, but also interact with their audience, receive feedback in real time, and build a community around their products or services. This two-way interaction creates a stronger bond between brands and their customers, increasing loyalty and trust.

Additionally, social media advertising allows for detailed measurement and analysis of campaign performance. Advertisers can track a variety of metrics, such as impressions, clicks, engagement rates, and conversions, allowing them to adjust their strategies in real time to optimize results. Platforms also offer advanced tools for testing different ad formats and messages to determine what resonates best with their audience.

In 2024, the trend is also towards the integration of social media advertising with other digital marketing channels. Brands often combine social media campaigns with SEO, email marketing, and other forms of online advertising to create a cohesive omnichannel experience for consumers.

In summary, social media advertising in 2024 is a dynamic and versatile tool, essential for brands looking to increase their visibility, engage their audience, and generate conversions. With its precise targeting capabilities, diverse format options, and potential for direct interaction with consumers, it represents a key component of any successful digital marketing strategy.

1.2.4. Trends and innovations

In 2024, the field of online advertising is marked by trends and innovations that redefine the way brands interact with their audiences. These developments are driven by technological advances, changes in consumer behavior and the need for greater personalization and efficiency in advertising campaigns.

One of the most significant trends is the increased use of artificial intelligence and machine learning. These technologies enable further personalization of advertising campaigns, analyzing large amounts of data to understand consumer preferences and behaviors. This allows advertisers to create advertising messages that resonate with each segment of their audience, increasing campaign effectiveness and improving user experience.

Augmented reality (AR) and virtual reality (VR) are also transforming online advertising. These technologies offer immersive and interactive experiences, allowing brands to stand out and create a strong emotional connection with consumers. For example, a fashion brand can use AR to allow customers to virtually try on clothes, while a tourism company can use VR to offer virtual tours of far-flung destinations.

Conversational marketing, thanks to chatbots and virtual assistants, is also gaining popularity. These tools enable real-time interaction with consumers, providing personalized customer service and improving engagement. Chatbots can answer questions, recommend products, and even process transactions, creating a seamless and interactive shopping experience.

Additionally, the rise of programmatic advertising continues to transform the advertising landscape. This approach uses algorithms to automatically buy advertising space, targeting specific audiences at the optimal time. This allows for greater efficiency and a better return on investment, as ads are more likely to reach people interested in the product or service offered.

Finally, ethics and transparency are becoming key

elements in online advertising. With increasing awareness of privacy issues and the use of personal data, brands are striving to be more transparent in their advertising practices. This includes complying with data protection regulations, such as GDPR, and communicating clearly about the use of consumer data.

These trends and innovations show that online advertising in 2024 is not just about selling products or services, but also about creating unique, personalized and ethical experiences for consumers. Brands that embrace these new technologies and approaches are better positioned to connect with their audiences in a meaningful and lasting way.

1.3 Social Networks

1.3.1. Dominant platforms in 2024

In 2024, the social media landscape is dominated by multiple platforms, each of which has evolved to meet the changing needs of users and advertisers. These platforms stand out for their unique features, target audiences, and abilities to engage users in innovative and meaningful ways.

Facebook continues to reign as a social media giant, with a massive and diverse user base. Its strength lies in its ability to connect people of all ages and backgrounds, providing brands with extensive and varied reach. Facebook has also integrated advanced augmented reality and e-commerce features, making the platform more immersive and interactive for users and more attractive to advertisers.

Instagram, with its focus on visual content, remains a platform of choice for aesthetic-focused brands, such as fashion, beauty and lifestyle. In 2024, Instagram strengthened its interface with augmented reality features and integrated shopping options, allowing users to interact with brands in a more dynamic and direct way.

TikTok, which has experienced a meteoric rise in recent years, continues to captivate a young and engaged audience. Its formula of short, creative and often viral content offers fertile ground for innovative and interactive advertising campaigns. TikTok has become a must-have for brands looking to reach Gen Z and tap into current cultural trends.

LinkedIn remains the dominant platform for professional networking and B2B marketing. In 2024, LinkedIn expanded its targeting and content capabilities, allowing businesses to connect with professionals and decision-makers more precisely and effectively. The platform is particularly valued for developing professional relationships and creating thought leadership content.

Finally, new emerging platforms, catering to specific niches or introducing new ways to connect online, are starting to gain traction. These platforms provide unique opportunities for brands to connect with specific audiences and explore new forms of content and engagement.

In summary, the dominant platforms in 2024 offer a diversity of channels and approaches for social media marketing. Each platform has unique characteristics that can be leveraged by brands to achieve their marketing goals, whether to increase brand awareness, engage with specific audiences, or generate direct sales. The key to success lies in understanding the strengths of each platform and adapting strategies to maximize impact with the target audience.

1.3.2. Content and engagement strategies

In 2024, social media content and engagement strategies have become more refined and user-centric, reflecting the ever-changing expectations and behaviors of online audiences. Brands that succeed in this space are those that understand the importance of creating meaningful and engaging content, tailored to the specifics of each platform and their target audience.

An effective content strategy starts with a deep understanding of the audience. Brands need to know who their followers are, what they care about, and how they interact with content across different platforms. This understanding allows you to create content that resonates with the audience, whether it's informative, entertainment, or inspirational posts. In 2024, the use of data analytics and artificial intelligence to understand user preferences and behaviors is common, enabling increased personalization and relevance of content.

Storytelling is another key element of content strategies. Captivating, well-told stories can create a strong emotional connection with the audience, increasing engagement and brand loyalty. Brands use stories to share their values, mission, and successes, transforming their content into immersive and memorable experiences for users.

Engagement is just as crucial as the content itself. Brands should be active and responsive on social media, responding to comments, participating in conversations, and encouraging users to interact with their content. Contests, surveys, and open-ended questions are effective ways to encourage interaction and create a community around the brand.

Video continues to be a dominant content format in 2024, with a preference for short, engaging, and easily consumable videos. Platforms like TikTok and Instagram Reels provide ideal opportunities for creative videos that can go viral. Brands are also leveraging live video for events, product launches, or Q&A sessions, providing a more authentic and personal experience.

Finally, adapting content to the specificities of each platform is essential. What works on Instagram may not work on LinkedIn or TikTok.

Brands must therefore adapt their message, tone and format depending on the platform and its audience. For example, content that is more formal and focused on thought leadership may be appropriate for LinkedIn, while content that is more visual and entertaining will be better suited for Instagram or TikTok.

In summary, content and engagement strategies in 2024 require a holistic approach that combines audience understanding, storytelling, active interaction, the use of varied content formats, and adaptation to different platforms . Brands that adopt these strategies are better positioned to create meaningful connections with their audiences, strengthen their online presence, and achieve their social media marketing goals.

1.3.3. Advertising and monetization

In 2024, social media advertising and monetization have reached new heights of innovation and effectiveness, providing brands and content creators with unprecedented opportunities to generate revenue. This evolution is the result of a better understanding of user behavior, the integration of advanced technologies, and the creation of more interactive and personalized advertising formats.

Social media advertising has become more sophisticated, with precise targeting options and diverse ad formats. Platforms like Facebook,

Instagram, and TikTok offer targeting tools based on demographics, interests, purchasing behaviors, and even previous interactions with the brand. This precision allows advertisers to deliver their messages to audiences most likely to be interested in their products or services, increasing conversion rates and ROI.

Advertising formats have also evolved, moving beyond traditional ads to include immersive experiences like augmented reality, interactive videos, and in-app stores. For example, augmented reality ads on Instagram allow users to virtually try on products, like glasses or makeup, creating an engaging and fun shopping experience. Similarly, interactive videos on TikTok invite users to participate in challenges or interact with content in creative ways, increasing engagement and brand visibility.

Monetization for content creators on social media has also gained momentum. Platforms like YouTube and Twitch have perfected their ad revenue sharing systems, giving creators a substantial share of the revenue generated by their videos. Additionally, features like Super Chats on YouTube and Bits on Twitch allow fans to financially support their favorite creators directly during live streams.

Brand partnerships and collaborations are another important source of income for creators. By working directly with brands to create sponsored content, influencers can generate revenue while providing their followers with relevant and authentic content. These partnerships have become more transparent and regulated, ensuring clear disclosure of sponsored collaborations to maintain trust and authenticity.

Finally, social media platforms have introduced new e-commerce features, allowing brands and creators to directly sell their products through their profiles and posts. These integrated shopping features transform social networks into comprehensive sales channels, providing a seamless and integrated shopping experience for users.

In conclusion, social media advertising and monetization in 2024 represents a dynamic and constantly evolving ecosystem, offering multiple opportunities for brands and content creators. With innovative advertising strategies, diverse monetization options, and increased e-commerce integration, social media has become powerful platforms for business growth and revenue generation.

1.3.4. Performance analysis and measurement

Analysis and measurement of performance on social networks in 2024 have become essential components of any digital marketing strategy. With platforms and user behaviors constantly evolving, understanding the impact and effectiveness of actions taken across these channels is crucial for brands and businesses. This in-depth understanding allows strategies to be adjusted in real time, resources to be optimized, and goals to be achieved more efficiently.

Social media platforms offer a wide range of built-in analytics tools that allow brands to track a variety of key metrics. These metrics include, but are not limited to, number of likes, shares, comments, post reach, engagement rate, and number of link clicks. This data provides valuable insights into how content is received by audiences, what type of content performs best, and when are the best times to post.

In 2024, social media analytics has become richer with the integration of artificial intelligence and machine learning. These technologies enable deeper analysis of trends, user sentiments, and interaction behaviors. For example, sentiment analysis can reveal how users perceive a brand or product, by examining the tone and context of comments and mentions on social media.

Brands also use third-party analytics tools to get more detailed insights and to combine data from different sources. These tools offer advanced features such as conversion tracking, user journey analysis, and audience segmentation. By combining social media data with other data sources, like website traffic or sales data, brands can get a holistic view of the effectiveness of their marketing efforts.

Analyzing social media performance is also essential for ROI (return on investment) and decision making. By measuring the effectiveness of advertising campaigns, content initiatives, and engagement strategies, businesses can determine which approaches provide the best ROI and adjust their budgets and resources accordingly.

Finally, analysis and performance measurement are not just post-campaign exercises, but ongoing processes. Brands must constantly monitor their social media performance to quickly detect emerging trends, respond to changes in user behaviors, and adjust their strategies in real time to stay relevant and effective.

In summary, analysis and measurement of performance on social networks in 2024 are key elements for understanding the impact of marketing actions, optimizing strategies, and guaranteeing maximum return on investment. With the advent of advanced technologies and the integration of diverse data, brands now have powerful tools to measure, analyze and continuously improve their presence on social networks.

CHAPTER 2: CONTENT STRATEGIES

"Your most unhappy customer is your best source of learning."
Bill Gates

2.1 Content Marketing

2.1.1 Creation of quality content

In the field of content marketing in 2024, the creation of quality content has become more than ever a cornerstone of brands' communication strategies. With consumer expectations constantly evolving and markets saturated, producing content that stands out for its quality, originality and relevance is essential to captivate attention and engage audiences.

Content quality is defined by several key criteria. First of all, authenticity and originality are essential. Consumers are constantly looking for content that provides a fresh perspective, is honest and reflects brand values. This means moving away from generic messages and creating content that tells a story, shares an experience or offers a unique insight.

Next, the relevance of the content is crucial. This means understanding the needs, interests and challenges of the target audience and creating content that meets them. In 2024, using data and analytics to understand audience preferences is common, allowing brands to personalize their messages and ensure their content is not only interesting, but also useful to their audience.

Content quality also requires excellent execution. This includes not only impeccable writing, but also the use of attractive visuals, engaging videos, and other multimedia elements. With the evolution of technologies and platforms, brands have a multitude of formats at their disposal to present their content in a creative and captivating way.

Additionally, the quality of content is closely linked to its ability to engage and drive action. Quality content should not only inform or entertain, but also encourage users to interact with the brand, whether through comments, shares, registrations or purchases. This requires a clear understanding of brand objectives and strategic integration of calls to action into content. Finally, content quality is an ongoing and evolving process. Brands must be willing to adapt, experiment and innovate with content to stay relevant in an ever-changing media landscape. This involves staying tuned to trends, gathering audience feedback, and adjusting content strategies accordingly.

In summary, creating quality content in 2024 is a complex mix of authenticity, relevance, excellence in execution, engagement and adaptability. Brands that succeed in this approach are those that understand and respect their audience, while being creative and innovative in the way they communicate their messages.

2.1.2 Distribution strategies

In 2024, content distribution strategies have become a crucial aspect of content marketing, requiring careful planning and strategic execution. With the abundance of content available online, it is no longer enough to create quality content; it is also essential to ensure that it reaches the target audience effectively. Content distribution involves a thorough understanding of the different channels available and how they can be used to maximize the reach and impact of content.

One of the keys to a successful distribution strategy is channel diversification. This includes not only traditional social networks like Facebook, Instagram, and Twitter, but also emerging platforms, blogs, email newsletters, and even podcasts. Each channel has its own strengths and attracts different audience segments. For example, social media is great for reaching a wide audience and encouraging engagement, while email newsletters are great for providing more in-depth content to an already interested audience.

Personalization of distribution is also essential. This means adapting the content and its format depending on the distribution channel. For example, long, detailed content may be better suited to a blog or newsletter, while a condensed, visually appealing version may be more effective on social media. This approach ensures that content is not only seen, but also engaging for the audience on each platform.

Another important strategy is the use of marketing automation and analytics tools to optimize distribution. These tools allow you to schedule the publication of content, target specific audiences, and monitor performance in real time. Analyzing performance data helps understand what type of content performs best on which channel, when to publish to maximize visibility, and how to adjust distribution strategies to improve engagement and reach.

Partnering with influencers and other brands can also be an effective way to distribute content. These partnerships help reach new audiences and add credibility to content. By collaborating with influencers or brands who share similar values, businesses can expand their reach organically and authentically.

Finally, it is crucial not to neglect the importance of SEO in content distribution. Optimizing content for search engines ensures long-term visibility and can lead to consistent organic traffic. This involves using relevant keywords, building internal and external links, and ensuring that content is easily accessible and indexable by search engines.

In summary, content distribution strategies in 2024 require a multi-channel, personalized and data-driven approach. By understanding the strengths of each channel, tailoring content to meet specific audience needs, and using analytics tools to optimize distribution, brands can ensure their quality content effectively reaches and engages their target audience.

2 1.3 Content marketing and SEO

In 2024, the interrelationship between content marketing and SEO is more pronounced and strategic than ever. This synergy is crucial to brands' online success because it combines the art of creating engaging, relevant content with the science of search engine optimization. This merger not only helps capture the attention of target audiences, but also ensures that content is easily discoverable and ranks well in search results.

Content marketing focuses on creating material that provides value to users, whether in the form of information, entertainment, or education. The goal is to create content that resonates with the audience, establishes brand credibility, and encourages engagement. However, no matter how good the content is, if it is not optimized for search engines, it may not reach its potential audience. This is where SEO comes into play.

SEO, or search engine optimization, involves adjusting various elements of content so that it is better understood and favored by search engines like Google. This includes strategically using relevant keywords, building internal and external links, optimizing meta tags and images, and ensuring content is structured in a way that it is easily indexable. When content marketing and SEO are aligned, content not only attracts the attention of readers, but is also well-positioned in search results, increasing its visibility and accessibility.

An effective strategy combines these two elements in a harmonious way. For example, when creating content, it is important to conduct keyword research to understand the terms and questions the target audience uses to search for information online. These keywords can then be integrated naturally into the content, ensuring that it not only meets user needs, but is also optimized for search engines.

Additionally, creating quality content that attracts

natural backlinks is another point of convergence between content marketing and SEO. Backlinks, or inbound links from other websites, are a key indicator of a site's quality and relevance to search engines. Engaging and informative content is more likely to be shared and referenced by other sites, which improves a site's backlink profile and, therefore, its ranking in search results.

Finally, it is essential to track and analyze content performance to understand how it is performing from both a content marketing and SEO perspective. This involves monitoring metrics such as website traffic, time on page, bounce rates, as well as keyword rankings and click-through rates (CTR) in search results. This data can provide valuable insights to refine and improve future strategies.

In conclusion, in 2024, content marketing and SEO are not isolated strategies, but interdependent components of an overall digital marketing strategy. Successfully integrating these two elements is essential to creating content that not only engages and informs users, but is also visible and ranked highly in search results, maximizing the reach and impact of online content.

2.1.4 Measuring effectiveness

Measuring content marketing effectiveness in 2024 is a complex and multidimensional process, essential for assessing the impact of content strategies and guiding future marketing decisions. With the evolution of technology and consumer behavior, brands have a wealth of data and tools to analyze the performance of their content. However, interpreting this data in a meaningful way is crucial to obtaining actionable insights and optimizing content strategies.

One of the first steps in measuring effectiveness is to set clear, measurable goals. These goals can vary depending on the needs of the brand and may include increasing website traffic, improving social media engagement, generating leads, or increasing sales. Once the objectives have been defined, it is important to choose relevant key performance indicators (KPIs) which will measure the achievement of these objectives. For example, if the goal is to increase engagement, KPIs could include the number of shares, comments and likes.

Web traffic analysis is a crucial aspect of measuring effectiveness. Web analytics tools, such as Google Analytics, provide detailed data on the number of visitors, session duration, bounce rates, and user journeys through the site. This data helps understand how users interact with content and what content attracts and retains visitors' attention.

Social media engagement is another important indicator of content effectiveness. Social media platforms offer their own analytics tools to track user engagement with content, including likes, shares, comments, and views. These metrics help assess how well content resonates with the audience and how well it encourages interaction.

Lead generation and conversions are also essential measures of effectiveness, especially for brands focused on business results. This involves tracking how content contributes to converting visitors into leads or customers. Using lead capture forms, specific landing pages, and tracking conversions are effective methods to measure this aspect.

Finally, it is important to carry out a qualitative content analysis. This includes collecting user feedback, analyzing comments, and assessing brand perception. These qualitative insights can complement quantitative data and provide a deeper understanding of the impact of content.

In conclusion, measuring content marketing effectiveness in 2024 requires a holistic approach that combines quantitative and qualitative analysis. By setting clear goals, choosing the right KPIs, and using a variety of tools and methods to analyze performance, brands can gain a deep understanding of the effectiveness of their content and optimize it to achieve their goals. marketing.

2.2 Storytelling and Personal Branding

2.2.1 The art of storytelling

In 2024, the art of storytelling has become a central element of personal branding and content marketing. Storytelling, or the art of telling stories, is a powerful technique that allows brands and individuals to connect emotionally with their audiences, convey messages in a memorable way, and stand out in a saturated media landscape.

Effective storytelling relies on creating a narrative that resonates with the audience. This involves weaving stories around values, experiences and emotions that are meaningful to the target audience. A good story should have a gripping beginning, an engaging development, and a satisfying conclusion. It must be authentic, creative and, above all, it must reflect the truth and values of the brand or person.

In the context of personal branding, storytelling is particularly powerful. It allows individuals to share their journey, challenges, successes and lessons in a way that inspires, educates and connects deeply with their audience. Whether it's an entrepreneur sharing the story of how they started their business, an artist discussing their inspirations, or a professional explaining their unique approach to their field, personal storytelling can transform the way others perceive a person and their brand .

Brands also use storytelling to bring their mission and values to life. Instead of focusing solely on the features or benefits of their products or services, they tell stories that illustrate the impact their brand has on people's lives. This could include stories from satisfied customers, stories behind a product's design, or initiatives that show the brand's commitment to social or environmental causes.

Storytelling in content marketing manifests itself through various formats - blogs, videos, podcasts, social networks, and even augmented and virtual reality. Each format offers a unique way to tell stories and reach audiences. For example, a video can capture visual and auditory emotions, while a blog can offer more detailed and thoughtful storytelling.

Finally, the art of storytelling in 2024 is enhanced by the use of data and analytics to understand what resonates with audiences. Brands and individuals can use user feedback and interactions to refine their stories, making them more relevant and impactful.

In summary, the art of storytelling is an essential skill in the world of marketing and personal branding in 2024. It helps create emotional connections, strengthen brand loyalty, and communicate messages in a powerful and memorable way. . Well-told stories have the power to captivate audiences, generate empathy and leave a lasting impression.

2.2.2 Building a personal brand

In 2024, building a personal brand has become an essential process for professionals in all sectors. A strong personal brand helps you stand out in a competitive market, establish a reputation for expertise and create career or business opportunities. The process of building a personal brand goes beyond simple self-promotion; it is about defining and communicating an authentic and coherent image of oneself.

The first step in building a personal brand is self-reflection. Understanding your own unique values, passions, skills and goals is crucial. This understanding helps define what sets an individual apart, what they can offer and what message they wish to convey. It's about creating a "personal story" that reflects not only professional skills, but also personality traits, life experiences and motivations.

Once this foundation is established, it is important to communicate this personal brand consistently across different channels. This includes professional social networks like LinkedIn, content platforms like blogs or YouTube, and network interactions. Every audience touchpoint should reinforce personal branding. For example, on social media, it is essential to share content that reflects the individual's expertise and interests, while actively engaging with the community to build relationships and credibility.

Content creation is a key part of building a personal brand. By sharing knowledge, ideas and experiences through articles, videos, podcasts or social media posts, an individual can demonstrate their expertise and passion. This content should be high quality, relevant to the target audience, and true to the person's voice and style.

Networking also plays a crucial role in building a personal brand. This involves connecting with professionals in the same industry, attending industry events, and collaborating with other professionals. Networking not only allows you to make yourself known, but also to learn from others, gain visibility and create opportunities for collaboration.

Finally, it's important to stay authentic and maintain a consistent online presence. The personal brand should be a true reflection of the individual, not a facade created to impress. Authenticity attracts trust and loyalty, and helps build lasting relationships with audiences.

In summary, building a personal brand in 2024 is a strategic process that involves understanding and communicating your unique value, creating and sharing relevant content, actively networking, and maintaining consistent authenticity. A strong personal brand can open doors, establish credibility, and create a lasting impact in an individual's professional career.

2.2.3 Examples of success

In 2024, there are many examples illustrating the remarkable success of personal brand building and effective storytelling. These examples serve as inspiring models for those looking to establish their own personal brand or improve their content strategy.

One prominent example is a tech entrepreneur who used his blog and YouTube channel to share his journey in growing his startup. By documenting the ups and downs of his entrepreneurial experience, he not only established his reputation as an expert in the technology field, but also created a loyal community of followers and future entrepreneurs. His videos, blending practical advice, lessons learned and personal insights, have attracted a wide audience, leading to mentoring opportunities, partnerships and even funding offers for his projects.

Another example is a dietitian who used Instagram and a blog to share nutritional tips, healthy recipes, and wellness information. By taking an authentic approach and sharing her own experiences with health challenges, she was able to establish a deep connection with her audience. His ability to present complex information in an accessible and engaging way has earned him a large fan base, as well as collaborations with health and wellness brands.

In the field of art, a photographer has brilliantly used social networks to exhibit his work. By sharing the story behind each photo, his techniques and inspirations, he not only showcased his artistry, but also created a captivating narrative that attracted the attention of art galleries and collectors. His skillful use of visual storytelling transformed his portfolio into an immersive experience, increasing his visibility and recognition in the art world.

A personal development coach also demonstrated the powerful impact of storytelling in building his brand. By sharing his personal experiences of overcoming obstacles and offering practical advice through podcasts and online seminars, he has established a strong brand based on inspiration and empowerment. His personal and sincere approach has helped many people achieve their personal and professional goals, further cementing his reputation as an influential coach.

These examples show that success in building a personal brand and storytelling depends not only on expertise in a specific field, but also on the ability to communicate authentically, create emotional connections and offer insight. the value to the audience. Whether through social media, blogs, videos or podcasts, effective storytelling and a well-defined personal brand can open doors to new opportunities and establish a lasting and influential presence in any field.

2.2.4 Tools and techniques

In 2024, a multitude of tools and techniques are available to help build and strengthen a personal brand and master the art of storytelling. These resources are essential for navigating the complex digital landscape and ensuring branding and communications efforts are effective and impactful.

Social media platforms remain essential tools for personal branding and storytelling. Each platform, whether it's LinkedIn, Instagram, Twitter, or TikTok, offers unique features that can be leveraged to achieve specific goals. LinkedIn, for example, is great for professional networking and sharing industry-related content, while Instagram and TikTok are great for visual and creative storytelling. Using these platforms strategically involves understanding their algorithms, leveraging their analytics tools to measure engagement, and creating content tailored to each specific audience.

Content creation tools like Canva, Adobe Creative Suite, and video editing software like Final Cut Pro or Adobe Premiere Pro are essential for producing high-quality visuals and videos. These tools allow you to create attractive designs, infographics, and captivating videos that can improve the visual impact of storytelling and make content more engaging.

Blogging platforms like WordPress and Medium provide a space to share more in-depth stories and feature articles. They are particularly useful for establishing expertise in a specific area and for providing in-depth information that cannot be fully explored within the confines of social media. For networking and relationship building, tools like LinkedIn Sales Navigator and customer relationship management (CRM) platforms are valuable. They allow you to track and analyze interactions with contacts, identify new networking opportunities, and maintain professional relationships.

Additionally, analytics and tracking tools, such as Google Analytics, Hootsuite, or Buffer, are crucial for measuring the effectiveness of content and personal branding. These tools provide insights into web traffic, social media engagement, and content performance, allowing strategies to be adjusted to maximize impact.

Podcasts and webinars are also effective techniques for storytelling and personal branding. They provide a way to share knowledge, ideas, and stories in a personal and engaging way. Podcasts, in particular, have grown in popularity as a way to build a loyal audience and establish a presence in a specific field.

In conclusion, in 2024, a diverse range of tools and techniques are available to professionals to build and strengthen their personal brand and storytelling. Effective use of these resources requires a clear understanding of brand objectives, knowledge of different platforms and technologies, and an ability to create content that resonates with the target audience. With the right tools and techniques, it is possible to create a strong personal brand and compelling storytelling that can open doors to new opportunities and establish an influential presence in any field.

2.3 Video Marketing

2.3.1. Importance of video marketing

In 2024, video marketing has established itself as a crucial element of any digital marketing strategy, playing a central role in the way brands communicate with their audiences. The importance of video marketing stems from its ability to captivate attention, convey complex messages in a concise and engaging manner, and generate deep emotional engagement.

One of the main reasons for the increased importance of video marketing is its ability to command attention in a crowded digital environment. With the abundance of content available online, videos stand out for their dynamism and ability to tell stories visually and aurally. They offer a more immersive experience than traditional content formats, like text or image, making them particularly effective at capturing and maintaining viewer interest.

Additionally, videos are an extremely versatile way to communicate information. They can be used for a variety of purposes, from product or service promotion to consumer education, brand building and community engagement. Videos help present complex concepts in a simple, understandable way, making them ideal for explaining technical products, demonstrating procedures, or telling a brand story.

The emotional impact of videos is also a key factor in their effectiveness. Videos can use elements such as music, dialogue, facial expressions and body language to create an emotional connection with the viewer. This ability to evoke emotions strengthens the impact of the message and can lead to greater brand loyalty and increased engagement.

Additionally, video marketing benefits from the ease of sharing on social media and other online platforms. Videos are often more likely to be shared than other types of content, increasing their reach and viral potential. This feature makes them particularly valuable for campaigns aimed at increasing brand awareness or reaching a large audience.

Finally, evolving technologies have made video production more accessible and affordable. With the advent of high-quality smartphones, video editing software, and live streaming platforms, it has become easier for brands of all sizes to create and distribute video content. This accessibility has opened the door to increased creativity and innovation in the field of video marketing.

In summary, the importance of video marketing in 2024 lies in its ability to capture attention, communicate effectively, establish an emotional connection, encourage sharing, and adapt to various marketing objectives. Brands that successfully integrate video marketing into their overall strategy can expect a significant improvement in engagement, awareness and the impact of their communications.

2.3.2. Video Content Strategies

In 2024, developing effective video content strategies has become an essential aspect of digital marketing. With online video consumption steadily increasing, brands need to take innovative and targeted approaches to stand out and engage their audiences. The key to success lies in creating video content that is not only captivating, but also aligned with brand goals and values.

The first step in developing a video content strategy is setting clear objectives. These goals can range from increasing brand awareness, audience engagement, lead generation, or sales conversion. A clear understanding of objectives helps guide the type of video content to produce, whether it's educational tutorials, customer testimonials, product demos, or inspiring brand stories.

Once the objectives are defined, it is crucial to understand the target audience. This involves knowing their preferences, their content consumption habits and the platforms they frequent. For example, a younger audience might be more engaged by short, dynamic videos on platforms like TikTok or Instagram, while a professional audience might prefer in-depth webinars or case studies on LinkedIn or YouTube.

Diversifying video formats is also an important component of a successful video content strategy. Brands should explore a variety of formats, such as live video, animation, interviews, explainer videos, and visual storytelling. Each format has its own strengths and can be used to communicate different aspects of the brand or achieve different goals.

Content quality is another crucial factor. In 2024, video production standards are high, and audiences expect visually appealing and technically well-produced content. This doesn't necessarily mean that each video needs to have a high production budget, but it should be well-designed, with good lighting, clear audio, and cohesive storytelling.

Optimizing videos for SEO (SEO) is also essential. This includes using relevant keywords in titles, descriptions and tags, as well as optimizing for mobile searches and different social media platforms. SEO helps ensure that videos are easily discoverable by target audiences.

Finally, measuring and analyzing video performance is essential to refine the video content strategy. Brands should track metrics like views, engagement rate, watch time, and conversions to evaluate the effectiveness of their videos. This data helps adjust future approaches and ensure videos continue to meet audience needs and interests.

In conclusion, an effective video content strategy in 2024 requires careful planning, audience understanding, format diversification, quality production, optimization for SEO, and continuous performance analysis. By adopting these approaches, brands can create videos that not only captivate and engage, but also significantly contribute to their overall marketing goals.

2.3.3. Platforms and formats

In 2024, the landscape of video marketing platforms and formats has diversified significantly, providing brands with a multitude of options to reach and engage their audiences. Each platform has unique characteristics and specific formats, suited to different types of content and audiences. Understanding these nuances is essential to maximizing the impact of video marketing strategies.

YouTube continues to dominate as the go-to video marketing platform, thanks to its vast audience and advanced SEO capabilities. This is a great place for longer, in-depth videos, such as tutorials, product demos, or webinars. YouTube is also effective for branded storytelling and video series, giving brands a space to build in-depth and engaging storytelling.

Instagram, with its emphasis on visuals, is perfect for short, punchy videos. Instagram Stories and Reels offer dynamic formats for quick, engaging content, ideal for capturing the attention of younger audiences. These formats are excellent for product previews, behind-the-scenes moments, or collaborations with influencers.

TikTok has revolutionized the video landscape with its short, viral video format. It's a key platform for reaching Generation Z and creating content that can quickly go viral. Brands are using TikTok for challenges, dance trends, and creative storytelling that encourage user engagement and the creation of user-generated content.

LinkedIn has established itself as a premier platform for professional and B2B video content. Videos on LinkedIn are ideal for sharing expert insights, case studies, and educational content that build brand credibility and authority in a professional context.

Outside of these core platforms, other emerging options offer unique opportunities. For example, platforms like Twitch or augmented/virtual reality applications open new avenues for immersive and interactive experiences.

As for the formats, they vary from live videos, which allow real-time interaction with the audience, to 360° videos which offer an immersive experience. Animated videos are also popular for explaining complex concepts in a simple and visually appealing way.

In conclusion, in 2024, the choice of video marketing platform and format must be aligned with the brand objectives, the content message, and the preferences of the target audience. A successful video marketing strategy often involves a combination of multiple platforms and formats, each contributing to a different aspect of brand storytelling and audience engagement. By wisely leveraging these various options, brands can create more dynamic, targeted and effective video marketing campaigns.

2.3.4 Impact measurement and ROI

In 2024, measuring the impact and return on investment (ROI) of video marketing campaigns has become standard practice for companies wishing to evaluate the effectiveness of their digital strategies. Understanding the true impact of videos on business and marketing objectives is crucial to justifying investments and guiding future strategic decisions.

The first step in measuring the impact of videos is to define key performance indicators (KPIs) aligned with the specific campaign objectives. These KPIs can include metrics such as number of views, engagement rate (likes, comments, shares), watch duration, and click-through rate on embedded links. For conversion-focused campaigns, KPIs such as conversion rate, number of leads generated, or sales directly attributable to the video are also important.

Analyzing these KPIs allows brands to understand not only how many people saw the video, but also how they interacted with it. For example, a high view rate but low engagement rate could indicate that the video is attracting attention but failing to encourage action. Likewise, a high number of clicks on an embedded link can indicate strong interest in the product or service presented.

To measure ROI, it is essential to relate these KPIs to the actual costs of video production and distribution. This involves taking into account creative costs, including production, editing, and possibly fees paid to influencers or agencies. By comparing these costs to the revenue generated or the value of leads obtained, businesses can calculate an accurate ROI and understand the financial effectiveness of their video campaigns.

Advanced analytics tools play a crucial role in measuring impact and ROI. Platforms like Google Analytics, integrated social media analytics tools, and specialized video marketing software offer detailed insights into video performance. These tools not only track standard KPIs, but also enable deeper analytics, such as user journey tracking, multi-touch attribution, and viewer behavior analysis.

Finally, it is important to take a holistic approach when measuring the impact of videos. This means considering not only quantitative metrics, but also qualitative impacts, such as improving brand awareness, consumer brand perception, and aligning video content with brand values. These qualitative aspects, although more difficult to measure, are essential to understanding the full impact of videos on the overall marketing strategy. In summary, measuring the impact and ROI of video marketing campaigns in 2024 requires a combination of KPI tracking, cost analysis, use of advanced analytics tools, and holistic evaluation qualitative impact. By taking this comprehensive approach, businesses can not only justify their video marketing investments, but also refine their strategies to maximize future impact.

CHAPTER 3: NEW TECHNOLOGIES AND DIGITAL MARKETING

"People don't believe in what you do, they believe in why you do it."

Simon Sinek

In 3.1 Artificial Intelligence and Automation

3.1.1 AI in digital marketing

In 2024, the integration of artificial intelligence (AI) into digital marketing has revolutionized the way businesses interact with their customers and optimize their marketing strategies. AI, with its advanced data analysis, machine learning and automation capabilities, has opened new avenues for personalization, efficiency and innovation in digital marketing.

One of the areas most impacted by AI in digital marketing is personalization at scale. Through complex data analysis and natural language processing, AI enables brands to create highly personalized user experiences. This manifests itself in product recommendations on e-commerce sites, personalized content in marketing emails, and targeted ads on social media. By understanding user preferences and behaviors, AI helps brands deliver the right message, to the right user, at the right time, thereby increasing engagement and conversion.

Automation, powered by AI, is another key area. Repetitive and time-consuming tasks, such as customer segmentation, sending emails, and managing advertising campaigns, can be automated using AI. This frees up valuable time for marketing teams, allowing them to focus on more strategic and creative aspects of marketing. Additionally, automation improves the efficiency and consistency of marketing campaigns, reducing human errors and ensuring fast and accurate execution.

AI also plays a crucial role in predictive analytics. By analyzing huge data sets, AI can identify trends, predict consumer behaviors, and anticipate future market needs. This capability allows businesses to make proactive, informed decisions, develop innovative products, and create marketing campaigns that meet changing consumer expectations.

Additionally, AI improves customer experience through chatbots and virtual assistants. These tools, powered by AI, offer real-time assistance, answer customer questions, and provide personalized support. This instant, personalized interaction improves customer satisfaction and strengthens brand loyalty.

Finally, AI helps optimize marketing campaigns in real time. Using machine learning, AI systems can continually learn from past interactions and adjust marketing strategies to maximize effectiveness. Whether it's adjusting bids for online ads or changing campaign content based on user feedback, AI ensures campaigns remain relevant and successful.

In conclusion, the integration of AI into digital marketing in 2024 has transformed the way businesses approach marketing. By offering advanced personalization, automation, predictive analytics, customer experience improvement, and real-time optimization capabilities, AI has become an indispensable tool for marketers looking to stay competitive in a constantly evolving digital environment.

3.1.2 Personalization and AI

In 2024, personalization in digital marketing has reached new heights thanks to the advanced integration of artificial intelligence (AI). AI has enabled personalization on a much deeper and more sophisticated level, transforming the way brands interact with their customers and delivering a highly personalized and relevant user experience.

AI allows businesses to collect and analyze massive amounts of data about user behaviors, preferences, and interactions. This in-depth analysis capability allows you to create detailed user profiles and understand the nuances of each individual's needs and desires. Using this information, brands can personalize their messages, offers, and content in a much more precise and relevant way for each user.

For example, in e-commerce, AI is used to recommend personalized products. By analyzing browsing behavior, previous purchases and product interactions, AI systems can suggest items that match customers' individual tastes and preferences. This approach is not limited to product recommendations; it also extends to personalizing the entire browsing experience, including site layout, displayed promotions, and even email communications.

In content, AI enables dynamic content personalization. AI systems can adjust the content displayed on a website or app in real time, based on user interactions. This means that each user receives a unique and personalized content experience, increasing engagement and relevance.

AI also plays a key role in personalizing advertising campaigns. By analyzing demographics, interests and online behaviors, AI can help target ads more precisely, ensuring messages reach the people most likely to be interested. This targeted approach not only improves the effectiveness of advertising campaigns, but also reduces the waste of advertising resources.

Additionally, AI improves customer experience through personalized interactions. AI-powered chatbots and virtual assistants can provide personalized customer support, answering customers' specific questions and offering recommendations based on their preferences and purchasing history.

In conclusion, personalization thanks to AI in 2024 has profoundly transformed digital marketing. It enables brands to create unique and relevant user experiences, improve customer engagement and satisfaction, and optimize the effectiveness of marketing campaigns. This advanced personalization is not only beneficial for brands in terms of increasing conversions and customer loyalty, but it also significantly improves the overall user experience.

3.1.3 Marketing automation

In 2024, marketing automation has become a fundamental part of digital marketing strategies, enabling businesses of all sizes to optimize their marketing efforts, improve efficiency, and personalize customer interactions at an unprecedented scale. previous. Marketing automation uses advanced technologies to manage and execute marketing tasks systematically and efficiently, thereby reducing manual workload and increasing campaign accuracy.

One of the biggest benefits of marketing automation is its ability to effectively manage customer interactions across various channels. This includes sending personalized emails, publishing content on social media, managing online advertising campaigns and updating websites. With automation, these tasks can be scheduled and executed automatically based on specific triggers or user behaviors, ensuring that the right message reaches the right customer at the right time.

Marketing automation is also essential for lead tracking and management. Automation systems can track user interactions with a company's website, emails and social media, recording valuable data about the interests and behaviors of potential customers. This information is then used to segment leads and further personalize marketing efforts, increasing the chances of conversion.

Additionally, marketing automation plays a crucial role in analytics and reporting. Automation tools provide detailed analytics on campaign performance, offering insights into aspects such as email open rate, click-through rate, website traffic and conversions. This data allows marketers to quickly adjust their strategies, optimize current campaigns and make informed decisions based on data.

The integration of artificial intelligence into marketing automation has also enabled significant advances in personalization and efficiency. AI can analyze large amounts of data to identify trends, predict customer behaviors, and automate complex marketing decisions. For example, AI can automatically recommend personalized products or services to individual customers, based on their purchasing history and preferences.

Finally, marketing automation makes messaging consistent and consistent across all channels. By centralizing campaign and content management, businesses can ensure their brand messaging remains consistent, regardless of customer touchpoint. This is essential to building a strong and reliable brand.

In conclusion, in 2024, marketing automation is an indispensable part of digital marketing, offering significant benefits in terms of efficiency, personalization, analysis and consistency of messages. By adopting automation, businesses can not only streamline their marketing operations but also deliver richer, more engaging customer experiences.

3.1.4 Application examples

In 2024, the application of artificial intelligence (AI) and automation in digital marketing has manifested itself through various innovative and impactful examples, demonstrating their ability to transform companies' marketing strategies.

A notable example is the use of AI-powered chatbots in customer service. These chatbots, integrated into websites and social media platforms, use natural language processing to understand and respond to customer queries in real time. For example, an e-commerce business might use a chatbot to help customers find products, answer questions about orders, or resolve customer service issues. These chatbots provide instant assistance, reduce waiting time for customers and free up human resources for more complex tasks.

Another example is automating email marketing campaigns. Automation systems use customer behavior data, like purchase history and previous email interactions, to send personalized messages. For example, after a customer purchases a product, AI can trigger a series of personalized emails offering complementary accessories or products, increasing the chance of additional sales.

AI is also used for content personalization on websites. Based on the user's browsing behavior, previous interactions and preferences, AI can dynamically change the content displayed on the website, creating a highly personalized experience. For example, a travel site may display personalized travel deals based on the user's previously viewed destinations or travel preferences.

In online advertising, AI and automation have enabled real-time optimization of advertising campaigns. AI algorithms continuously analyze ad performance and automatically adjust bidding, targeting and content to maximize ROI. For example, a social media advertising campaign can be constantly adjusted based on user interactions, ensuring that ads are always relevant and effective.

Finally, AI-based predictive analytics is used to anticipate market trends and consumer behavior. By analyzing large amounts of data, businesses can predict future customer needs, identify emerging market opportunities, and adjust their strategies accordingly. For example, a fashion brand can use predictive analytics to anticipate fashion trends and adjust its collections and inventory accordingly.

These examples illustrate how AI and automation are transforming digital marketing in 2024, delivering more personalized customer experiences, optimizing marketing operations and providing valuable insights for decision-making. Adopting these technologies allows businesses to remain competitive in an ever-changing digital landscape and deliver exceptional customer experiences.

3.2 Augmented and Virtual Reality

3.2.1 AR/VR in marketing

In 2024, augmented reality (AR) and virtual reality (VR) have taken a leading role in digital marketing, offering immersive and interactive experiences that redefine customer engagement. The adoption of these technologies has enabled brands to create innovative advertising campaigns, improve the shopping experience and strengthen the emotional connection with consumers.

AR, in particular, has revolutionized the retail industry. Brands are using AR to allow customers to virtually try products before purchasing. For example, a cosmetics brand might offer an AR application that allows users to see how different makeup products would look on their face in real time. Similarly, furniture stores are using AR to help customers visualize how furniture would fit into their living space. These immersive shopping experiences not only improve customer satisfaction but also reduce return rates by providing a better understanding of the product.

In VR, brands are creating complete brand experiences that immerse users in fully designed worlds. For example, an automobile company can use VR to offer customers a virtual driving experience of their latest car model. Travel and tourism companies are using VR to offer virtual tours of destinations, allowing customers to experience travel before booking. These VR experiences are not only engaging, but they also help build anticipation and desire for the product or service.

AR and VR are also used for interactive advertising campaigns. Brands are creating ads where users can interact with AR elements or immerse themselves in VR experiences. These campaigns don't just capture attention; they create lasting memories and build brand engagement.

Additionally, these technologies offer unique opportunities for brand storytelling. By using AR and VR, businesses can tell stories in a more immersive and emotional way. For example, a brand can use VR to transport users into the story of the company's founding or to show the impact of its sustainability initiatives.

Finally, AR and VR provide valuable data on user behavior. Brands can track how users interact with AR/VR experiences, which products they prefer, and how much time they spend with certain features. This data can be used to refine marketing strategies and improve future experiences.

In conclusion, the integration of AR and VR in digital marketing in 2024 has opened up new dimensions of customer engagement. By offering immersive shopping experiences, interactive advertising campaigns, captivating storytelling opportunities and valuable behavioral insights, AR and VR enable brands to connect with consumers in a deeper and more meaningful way.

3.2.2 Innovative campaigns

In 2024, the use of augmented reality (AR) and virtual reality (VR) in marketing campaigns has resulted in remarkably innovative advertising initiatives, transforming the way brands interact with their audiences. These technologies have helped create immersive and memorable advertising experiences, which not only captivate consumers' attention, but also strengthen brand engagement.

A striking example of an innovative campaign is a fashion brand that launched an AR experience allowing users to virtually view and try on clothing and accessories via their smartphone. This campaign not only generated considerable buzz due to its innovative nature, but also increased conversion rates by providing customers with a more interactive and personalized shopping experience.

In the entertainment industry, a major film production company used VR to create an immersive experience tied to the release of a highly anticipated film. Users could explore scenes from the film, interact with story elements, and even take part in virtual missions. This campaign not only drove interest in the film, but also delivered a deep and engaging brand experience that strengthened fan loyalty.

An automotive company innovated by using VR to offer virtual test drives of its new models. Customers could sit in a VR simulator and experience a realistic driving experience, including the feeling of driving on different terrains and in various weather conditions. This approach not only overcame the limitations of traditional test drives, but also allowed the brand to stand out in a competitive market.

In the education and training space, a technology company launched a VR campaign aimed at educating the public about new technologies. Users could participate in interactive simulations to learn how these technologies work and their potential impact on society. This campaign not only strengthened the company's position as a leader in technological innovation, but also helped educate and engage the public on important topics.

Finally, a beauty brand used AR to create an interactive social media campaign, where users could virtually try on different makeup products. By sharing their virtual looks on social media, users could enter a competition, increasing brand visibility and encouraging consumer engagement. These examples illustrate how AR and VR can be used to create marketing campaigns that are not only innovative, but also deeply engaging. By providing immersive and interactive experiences, these technologies enable brands to connect with their audiences in more meaningful ways, build brand awareness, and increase customer engagement and loyalty.

3.2.3 Integration with social networks

In 2024, the integration of augmented reality (AR) and virtual reality (VR) with social media has opened up new avenues for digital marketing, creating more immersive and interactive user experiences. This convergence has allowed brands to connect with their audiences in more meaningful ways, transforming the way users interact with content on social platforms.

The integration of AR into social networks has notably revolutionized user engagement. Platforms like Instagram and Snapchat have adopted AR to allow users to have interactive experiences directly from their app. For example, beauty brands use AR filters to allow users to virtually try on makeup products, while fashion retailers offer virtual clothing try-ons. These AR experiences don't just increase user engagement; they also provide valuable insight into consumer preferences, which is essential for targeted marketing strategies.

VR, although less prevalent on social media due to its more immersive nature and the need for specific equipment, has also found its place. Platforms like Facebook Horizon and other VR social spaces allow users to immerse themselves in virtual environments where they can interact with brand content in deeper ways. For example, a travel company can create a VR experience where users can virtually explore a destination, providing a unique form of storytelling and promotion.

The integration of AR and VR with social media has also paved the way for more innovative and engaging advertising campaigns. Brands can create interactive AR ads that encourage users to interact with the product in a fun way, thereby increasing brand awareness and consumer engagement. Likewise, VR experiences shared on social media can generate buzz and encourage content sharing, expanding brand reach.

Additionally, integrating these technologies with social media allows for increased personalization of marketing. Using data collected from user interactions with AR and VR experiences, brands can refine their marketing and content strategies to better meet the interests and needs of their target audience.

In conclusion, the integration of AR and VR with social media in 2024 has significantly enriched user experience and offered brands new ways to connect with their audiences. By creating immersive and interactive experiences, brands can not only increase engagement and awareness, but also gain valuable insights into their consumers' preferences, which is essential for digital marketing success in the modern era.

3.2.4 Future of AR/VR in marketing

In 2024, the future of augmented reality (AR) and virtual reality (VR) in marketing looks bright and full of potential. These technologies continue to evolve at a rapid pace, opening new possibilities for brands to create immersive and memorable customer experiences. The impact of AR and VR in marketing extends far beyond simple technological gadgets; they are becoming essential tools for brand storytelling, customer engagement and marketing personalization.

One of the most significant developments expected in the future of AR and VR is their further integration into consumers' daily lives. As technology improves and costs drop, it is expected that more people will have access to these experiences. This means brands will be able to reach a wider and more diverse audience, delivering AR and VR experiences in increasingly varied contexts, from physical stores to online platforms.

Another important aspect of the future of AR and VR in marketing is improved personalization. Thanks to advances in AI and machine learning, AR and VR experiences will be able to be tailored to users' individual preferences, providing an even more personalized and relevant experience. For example, an in-store AR experience could recommend specific products based on the customer's purchase history, while a VR experience could adapt in real time to user reactions and interactions.

The future will also see deeper integration of AR and VR into omnichannel strategies. Brands will look to create consistent and connected experiences across different customer touchpoints, whether physical stores, websites, mobile apps or social media. This omnichannel approach will create a seamless and integrated customer journey, strengthening engagement and brand loyalty.

Additionally, the future of AR and VR in marketing could see the emergence of new forms of advertising and brand partnerships. For example, brands could collaborate with VR gaming platforms to create immersive brand experiences, or use AR to deliver interactive, personalized ads in urban environments.

Finally, it is likely that ethical and privacy issues will play an increasingly important role in the use of AR and VR in marketing. Brands will need to be mindful of how they collect and use user data, and ensure that AR and VR experiences respect consumer privacy and security.

In conclusion, the future of AR and VR in marketing is full of possibilities. These technologies provide brands with unique opportunities to innovate their marketing strategies, create compelling customer experiences, and build brand engagement and loyalty. However, to take full advantage of these opportunities, brands will need to navigate an ever-changing landscape, remaining attentive to technological advances, consumer expectations and ethical considerations.

3.3 Blockchain and Marketing

3.3.1 Blockchain explained

In 2024, blockchain has become a household term, but its understanding often remains limited to the field of cryptocurrencies. However, blockchain has much greater potential, particularly in digital marketing. At its core, blockchain is a distributed ledger technology that allows data to be stored securely, transparently and unalterably. This technology works like a blockchain (hence the name), where each block contains a set of transactions or information, cryptographically linked to the previous block, thus forming a chain. One of the main strengths of blockchain is its decentralized nature. Unlike traditional databases managed by a central entity, blockchain is distributed across a network of computers, making data both more secure and resistant to manipulation. Every transaction on the blockchain is verified by network consensus, which guarantees the authenticity and reliability of the information recorded.

In the context of marketing, blockchain offers several advantages. First, it ensures increased transparency. Businesses can use blockchain to create a transparent and verifiable history of their products, from production to delivery. This can be particularly useful for brands that want to prove the authenticity of their products or demonstrate their commitment to ethical and sustainable practices.

Second, blockchain offers improved possibilities for data security. In a world where consumer data protection is of increasing concern, blockchain can offer a more secure solution for storing and managing customer data. This can help build consumer trust in brands that use this technology.

In addition, blockchain facilitates the implementation of smart contracts. These self-executing contracts, which activate when certain conditions are met, can automate various aspects of marketing and sales, such as managing loyalty rewards, verifying copyrights or implementing loyalty programs. affiliation.

Finally, blockchain opens the way to new forms of advertising and promotion. For example, it can be used to create transparent and secure reward systems for consumers who share their data or participate in advertising campaigns.

In summary, blockchain in marketing goes well beyond cryptocurrencies. It offers innovative possibilities for transparency, data security, process automation and the creation of new marketing strategies. As technology continues to evolve, its potential in marketing only grows, providing businesses with unique opportunities to connect with their customers in a more secure and engaging way.

3.3.2 Applications in marketing

In 2024, blockchain has found revolutionary applications in marketing, transforming the way businesses interact with consumers and manage data. The use of this technology in digital marketing not only provides greater transparency and security, but also paves the way for more innovative and effective marketing methods.

One of the most notable applications of blockchain in marketing is loyalty and rewards management. Blockchain-based loyalty programs allow businesses to create transparent and secure reward systems. Consumers can accumulate and redeem loyalty points more efficiently, with the assurance that their data and transactions are secure and immutable. This approach builds customer trust and improves their engagement with the brand.

Blockchain is also used to provide supply chain transparency, which is particularly relevant for brands focused on sustainability and ethics. Businesses can use blockchain to record and track the origin and journey of their products, from source to sale. This transparency allows consumers to verify the authenticity of products and the company's sustainable practices, thereby building trust and brand loyalty.

In the field of digital advertising, blockchain offers solutions to combat advertising fraud and improve the transparency of advertising transactions. By using blockchain, businesses can ensure that their ads are served securely and that impression and click data is reliable and tamper-proof. This allows for better optimization of advertising campaigns and more efficient allocation of advertising budgets.

Blockchain also facilitates the implementation of smart contracts in marketing campaigns. These automated contracts can be used to manage deals with influencers, co-marketing partnerships or affiliate programs. Smart contracts ensure that all parties honor their commitments and that payments or rewards are distributed automatically once conditions are met, thereby simplifying processes and reducing the risk of non-compliance.

In addition, blockchain allows for more secure management of customer data. In a context where the protection of personal data has become a major concern, blockchain offers a solution for storing and managing data in a secure and transparent manner. This can help businesses comply with data protection regulations while building consumer trust.

In conclusion, the applications of blockchain in digital marketing in 2024 are vast and varied. From loyalty program management to supply chain transparency, combating ad fraud and secure data management, blockchain offers businesses powerful tools to improve their marketing strategies, build trust consumers and optimize the effectiveness of their campaigns. As technology continues to develop, its potential in digital marketing will only grow, providing even more innovative opportunities for brands.

3.3.3 Transparency and security

In 2024, transparency and security in digital marketing have taken on increased importance, and blockchain is at the heart of this evolution. Blockchain's unique ability to provide unparalleled transparency and enhanced security has transformed the way businesses manage data and interact with consumers.

Transparency is one of the main benefits of blockchain in marketing. Thanks to its distributed and immutable ledger, each transaction or interaction recorded on the blockchain is transparent and verifiable by all network participants. This feature is particularly beneficial for brands keen to demonstrate their commitment to ethical and sustainable practices. For example, a company can use blockchain to trace the origin and journey of its products, providing consumers with the ability to verify product authenticity and brand sustainability claims. This transparency builds consumer trust and improves brand image.

In terms of security, blockchain offers a higher level of data protection than traditional methods. Data stored on the blockchain is encrypted and distributed across a decentralized network, making it virtually tamper-proof. This enhanced security is essential in a context where data breaches and privacy concerns are commonplace. Businesses can store customer data securely on the blockchain, ensuring sensitive information is protected and building customer trust.

Blockchain also contributes to security and transparency in the field of digital advertising. It helps fight ad fraud by providing a transparent and tamper-proof record of ad impressions, clicks and conversions. This allows advertisers to ensure that their advertising budgets are spent efficiently and that campaign results are authentic. This transparency also helps build trust between advertisers, publishers and consumers.

Additionally, blockchain facilitates the implementation of smart contracts in marketing campaigns. These automated contracts, executed on the blockchain, ensure that all parties respect their commitments. For example, in an affiliate campaign, a smart contract can automatically trigger a payment once a sale is confirmed, ensuring fair and transparent compensation for all parties involved.

In conclusion, the transparency and security brought by blockchain in digital marketing in 2024 are major assets for businesses. By adopting this technology, brands can not only build consumer trust but also improve the effectiveness and authenticity of their marketing campaigns. Blockchain offers a robust solution for navigating a digital landscape where data protection and transparency of operations are increasingly valued by consumers and regulators.

3.3.4 Case studies

In 2024, several case studies illustrate the revolutionary impact of blockchain on digital marketing, demonstrating how different companies have adopted this technology to improve the transparency, security and effectiveness of their marketing strategies.

A notable case study is that of a major luxury goods brand that used blockchain to combat counterfeiting and build consumer trust. The brand has integrated blockchain technology to create a traceability system for its products, from manufacturing to sale. Each product was accompanied by a digital certificate stored on the blockchain, guaranteeing its authenticity. This initiative not only helped protect the brand against counterfeiting, but also increased consumer confidence in the authenticity and quality of the products.

Another example is a company in the food industry that used blockchain to provide transparency in its supply chain. The company recorded all stages of the production, transportation and distribution of its products on a publicly accessible blockchain. Consumers could scan a QR code on products to access the complete supply chain history. This transparency has not only improved consumer trust, but also allowed the company to stand out in a market increasingly focused on sustainability and ethics.

In the digital advertising industry, an innovative campaign used blockchain to create a transparent and secure reward system for users who share their data. Users could choose to share some of their data in exchange for blockchain tokens, which could be used for purchases or services within the brand's ecosystem. This approach allowed the company to collect valuable data while respecting users' privacy and rewarding them for their participation.

Another case study concerns a technology company that implemented smart contracts to manage its affiliate partnerships. Smart contracts automated the commission payment process, ensuring that affiliates were paid fairly and transparently based on sales made. This automation not only reduced administrative costs, but also strengthened partner relationships through greater transparency and reliability.

Finally, an entertainment company used blockchain to create a unique fan experience. Fans could purchase blockchain tokens that gave them access to exclusive content, special events and direct interactions with artists. This strategy not only generated new revenue streams for the company, but also created a more engaged and loyal fan community.

These case studies demonstrate the versatility and effectiveness of blockchain in various aspects of digital marketing. From product traceability to consumer data management, advertising and fan engagement, blockchain offers businesses innovative ways to improve the transparency, security and efficiency of their marketing operations. As technology continues to evolve, its potential in marketing only grows, providing ever more innovative opportunities for brands.

CHAPTER 4:
ANALYSIS AND
DATA SCIENCE

"Creativity is just about connecting things. When you ask creative people how they did something, they feel a little guilty because they didn't really do it, they just saw something."

Steve Jobs

4.1 Big Data in Digital Marketing

4.1.1 Introduction to Big Data

In 2024, Big Data has become an essential part of digital marketing, playing a crucial role in how businesses understand, interact with, and respond to their customers. The term "Big Data" refers to extremely large data sets that are analyzed by advanced technologies to reveal trends, patterns, and associations, particularly with respect to human behavior and interactions.

The introduction of Big Data in digital marketing has marked a significant transformation in business decision-making and strategy. With access to a massive amount of information from a variety of sources – social media, online transactions, mobile data, and more – businesses can now gain a deep understanding of their customers' needs, preferences, and behaviors. This wealth of information allows marketers to create more targeted campaigns, personalize customer experiences, and optimize marketing strategies for maximum effectiveness.

Big Data in digital marketing is not limited to collecting large amounts of data; it is also about the ability to analyze and interpret this data to derive actionable insights. The use of advanced analytics tools, artificial intelligence and machine learning enables businesses to quickly process and analyze large volumes of data, transforming raw information into valuable insights.

This data-driven approach enables more precise market segmentation, better understanding of the customer journey and real-time optimization of marketing campaigns. For example, by analyzing user behavior data on a website, a business can identify friction points in the purchasing journey and make improvements to increase conversion rates.

Additionally, Big Data plays a key role in predicting future consumer trends and behaviors. By identifying patterns in historical data, businesses can anticipate future customer needs, adapt their products and services accordingly, and stay ahead of the competition.

In conclusion, Big Data has radically changed the digital marketing landscape, providing businesses with unprecedented opportunities to effectively understand and respond to their customers. By harnessing the power of Big Data, businesses can not only improve their marketing strategies, but also strengthen their market position and create more enriching and personalized customer experiences.

4.1.2 Data collection and management

In 2024, data collection and management as part of Big Data have become crucial aspects of digital marketing, requiring meticulous and strategic attention. A company's ability to efficiently collect relevant data and manage it responsibly and efficiently is essential to realizing the full potential of Big Data.

Data collection in digital marketing takes place across a multitude of channels. Businesses collect information from user interactions on websites, mobile apps, social media, online transactions, and even connected devices as part of the Internet of Things (IoT). Each interaction provides valuable data that can include information about browsing habits, purchasing preferences, search behaviors, and reactions to marketing campaigns. To maximize the efficiency of data collection, companies use advanced tools such as cookies, tracking pixels, and web analytics software.

However, simply collecting data is not enough. Effective management of this data is equally crucial. This involves organizing, storing and analyzing collected data so that it is accessible, usable and secure. Businesses need to implement robust data management systems that can store large amounts of data while ensuring its integrity and confidentiality. This includes the use of scalable databases, cloud storage solutions, and data management systems that enable rapid access and analysis of data.

Data security is another crucial aspect of data management. With data privacy concerns increasing and strict regulations such as GDPR in place, businesses must ensure that data is collected, stored and used in a compliant and secure manner. This involves implementing robust security protocols, data encryption, and clear data privacy policies.

Additionally, data quality is essential for accurate analyses. Businesses must have processes in place to clean and validate data, eliminating duplicates, correcting errors, and ensuring data is up-to-date and accurate. Good data quality ensures that insights from analytics are reliable and relevant.

Finally, data management also involves analyzing and interpreting data to derive actionable insights.

Businesses use advanced data analytics tools, including artificial intelligence and machine learning, to analyze trends, identify patterns, and predict consumer behaviors. These analytics enable businesses to make informed decisions, personalize customer experiences and optimize marketing strategies.

In conclusion, the collection and management of data within the framework of Big Data are fundamental elements of digital marketing in 2024. Effective data management allows companies to maximize the use of collected information, improve decision-making , strengthen security and compliance, and deliver more personalized and engaging customer experiences.

4.1.3 Data analysis for marketing

In 2024, data analytics has become a central pillar of digital marketing, enabling businesses to transform huge volumes of raw data into valuable, actionable insights. This ability to analyze and interpret data is crucial to understanding consumer behaviors, optimizing marketing strategies and improving business results.

Data analytics in digital marketing involves the use of sophisticated techniques and tools to examine data collected from various sources. This includes web browsing data, social media interactions, purchase histories, responses to advertising campaigns, and much more. By analyzing this data, businesses can identify trends, behavior patterns, consumer preferences and market opportunities. For example, analyzing clickstream data can reveal the most common paths customers take through a website, helping to optimize user experience and increase conversion rates.

One of the most powerful aspects of data analysis is market segmentation. By segmenting consumers into groups based on criteria such as age, gender, geographic location, interests and purchasing behaviors, businesses can create targeted and personalized marketing campaigns. This targeted approach is not only more cost effective, but it also increases the relevance and effectiveness of marketing messages, improving customer engagement and loyalty.

Predictive analytics, a branch of data analytics, also plays a crucial role in digital marketing. Using statistical models and machine learning algorithms, businesses can predict future trends, consumer behaviors and marketing campaign results. For example, predictive analytics can help anticipate which products a customer is likely to purchase next, allowing businesses to provide personalized and timely recommendations.

Additionally, data analytics helps measure and optimize the return on investment (ROI) of marketing campaigns. By tracking key metrics like click-through rate, conversion rate, cost per acquisition, and customer lifetime value, businesses can evaluate the effectiveness of their campaigns and adjust their strategies to maximize ROI. This data-driven approach ensures that marketing resources are allocated in a way that generates the best possible return.

Finally, data analysis enables faster and more informed decision-making. With access to real-time insights, businesses can respond quickly to market changes, consumer behaviors and campaign performance. This agility is essential in an ever-changing business environment, where the ability to adapt quickly can be a key success factor.

In conclusion, data analytics for marketing in 2024 is a dynamic and essential field, enabling businesses to effectively navigate the complex digital marketing landscape. By transforming data into valuable insights, businesses can create more targeted, personalized and effective marketing strategies, improving customer engagement and business results.

4.1.4 Privacy and ethics

In 2024, privacy and ethical considerations associated with data analysis in digital marketing have become major areas of concern for businesses and consumers. With the increase in big data collection and analysis, it is imperative that businesses approach these issues responsibly to maintain consumer trust and comply with current regulations.

Consumer privacy is at the heart of ethical concerns related to data analysis. Companies must ensure that personal data is collected, stored and used in a way that respects the privacy of individuals. This involves implementing robust security protocols to protect data from unauthorized access or breaches, and ensuring that data is encrypted and secure. Additionally, companies must be transparent about how data is collected and used, and obtain explicit consent from consumers for its processing.

Compliance with data protection regulations, such as the European Union's General Data Protection Regulation (GDPR) or the California Consumer Privacy Act (CCPA), is also essential. These regulations impose strict requirements on the handling of personal data, including the right for consumers to know what data is collected about them, to request deletion of their data, and to opt out of its use for marketing purposes. Businesses must ensure they are fully compliant with these regulations to avoid significant penalties and preserve their reputation.

Furthermore, ethical considerations go beyond simple legal compliance. Businesses must take an ethical approach to their use of data, ensuring that insights gained from data analysis are not used to manipulate or exploit consumers. This includes avoiding practices such as overly intrusive targeting, data-based discrimination, or using sensitive data unethically.

The importance of ethics in data analysis is also linked to building consumer trust. In an environment where concerns about privacy and data security are high, companies that demonstrate a commitment to ethical and responsible practices can differentiate themselves and build customer loyalty.

In conclusion, privacy and ethics in data analysis for digital marketing in 2024 are essential aspects that businesses must address seriously. By adopting responsible and compliant data management practices, and committing to using data ethically and transparently, businesses can not only comply with regulations, but also build customer trust and loyalty.

4.2 Predictive and Behavioral Analysis

4.2.1 Foundations of predictive analytics

In 2024, predictive analytics has become an essential tool in the field of digital marketing, allowing businesses to predict future trends, consumer behaviors and campaign results. Based on the use of data, statistics and machine learning models, predictive analytics helps businesses anticipate customer needs and wants, optimize marketing strategies and make informed decisions.

Predictive analytics relies on the collection and analysis of large amounts of historical and current data. This data can include information about customer transactions, website and social media interactions, purchasing habits, and even external data such as economic trends or weather conditions. By analyzing this data, businesses can identify patterns and trends that help them understand past and current consumer behavior.

Once these patterns are identified, predictive analytics uses various statistical and machine learning techniques to create predictive models. These models are able to predict future results based on historical data. For example, a predictive model can be used to anticipate which customers are likely to respond positively to a certain marketing campaign, what the odds are of churning from a service, or which products a customer is likely to purchase next.

One of the key benefits of predictive analytics is its ability to help businesses make proactive rather than reactive decisions. Instead of waiting for trends to emerge, businesses can use predictive analytics to anticipate market changes and adjust their strategies accordingly. This can lead to better resource allocation, more targeted marketing campaigns and an overall improvement in operational efficiency.

Additionally, predictive analytics plays a crucial role in marketing personalization. By understanding individual customer behaviors and preferences, businesses can create personalized experiences that increase customer engagement and loyalty. For example, by predicting a customer's product preferences, a business can personalize its product recommendations, providing a more relevant and satisfying shopping experience.

In conclusion, the foundations of predictive analytics in digital marketing in 2024 lie in the ability to transform large amounts of data into valuable and predictive insights. By anticipating future trends and understanding consumer behaviors, businesses can optimize their marketing strategies, deliver personalized customer experiences, and stay competitive in an ever-changing marketplace.

4.2.2 Understanding consumer behavior

In 2024, understanding consumer behavior has become a fundamental aspect of digital marketing, allowing businesses to create more effective and personalized strategies. Consumer behavior analysis involves the in-depth study of customer actions, motivations, preferences and purchasing decisions, using a combination of quantitative and qualitative data.

Analyzing consumer behaviors begins with collecting data across various touchpoints. This includes interactions on websites, mobile applications, social networks, physical points of sale and customer service interactions. This data provides valuable insights into how consumers interact with the brand, the products they prefer, the paths they take before making a purchase, and the factors that influence their purchasing decisions.

Using advanced analytics tools allows businesses to decipher these vast data sets to identify trends and patterns. For example, analyzing website clickstreams can reveal key stages where customers abandon their shopping cart, while analyzing social media interactions can provide insights into consumer attitudes and perceptions towards the brand.

In addition to quantitative data, understanding consumer behavior also involves analyzing qualitative data, such as customer reviews, reviews, and feedback. This qualitative information provides deeper insight into customer motivations, needs and concerns, complementing quantitative data to create a complete picture of consumer behavior.

Behavioral analytics also helps segment customers into distinct groups based on their behaviors, preferences, and demographics. This segmentation allows businesses to target their marketing messages more precisely, creating campaigns that resonate with the specific needs and desires of each segment.

Additionally, understanding consumer behavior is essential for personalization. By identifying individual preferences and purchasing behaviors, businesses can personalize their offers, recommendations and communications for each customer. This personalized approach not only increases the effectiveness of marketing campaigns, but also improves the customer experience, thereby strengthening loyalty and satisfaction.

In conclusion, understanding consumer behavior in 2024 is crucial for digital marketing success. By combining quantitative and qualitative data analysis, businesses can gain a deeper understanding of their customers, allowing them to create more targeted, personalized and effective marketing strategies. This customer-centric approach is essential to building lasting relationships and remaining competitive in an ever-changing market.

4.2.3 Tools and techniques

In 2024, a diverse range of tools and techniques are used to carry out predictive and behavioral analysis in digital marketing. These tools and techniques enable businesses to effectively collect, analyze and interpret data to understand and anticipate consumer behaviors.

Advanced data analytics tools are at the heart of predictive and behavioral analytics. Platforms like Google Analytics, Adobe Analytics, and other specialized tools provide detailed insights into user behavior online. These tools allow you to track user journeys on websites, analyze conversion rates, measure engagement on different pages and understand navigation patterns. They also offer advanced segmentation features, allowing businesses to target specific groups of customers based on their behavior.

Artificial intelligence (AI) and machine learning are also essential components of predictive analytics. These technologies allow businesses to process large amounts of data and identify complex patterns that would be difficult to detect manually. For example, machine learning algorithms can predict future customer behaviors, such as purchase or churn probabilities, based on historical data.

Customer relationship management (CRM) tools play a crucial role in behavioral analysis. These systems help businesses collect and manage detailed information about their customers, including past interactions, preferences and purchasing histories. By integrating CRM data with analytics tools, businesses can get a 360-degree view of their customers, which is essential for effective personalization.

Social media platforms and social media analytics tools also provide valuable data for behavioral analysis. These tools allow businesses to monitor brand mentions, analyze user sentiment, and track trends on social media. These insights help businesses understand consumer attitudes and perceptions towards their brand and products.

Finally, data visualization techniques are used to present the results of the analysis in an understandable and actionable way. Tools like Tableau, Qlik, or Microsoft Power BI allow businesses to create interactive dashboards and visual reports, making it easier to interpret data and make data-driven decisions.

In conclusion, the tools and techniques for predictive and behavioral analytics in 2024 are varied and sophisticated, ranging from data analytics and CRM tools to AI and machine learning, social media tools and data visualization. Effective use of these tools allows businesses to deeply understand their customers, predict future trends, and create more targeted and personalized marketing strategies.

4.2.4 Case studies

In 2024, several case studies illustrate the significant impact of predictive and behavioral analytics in digital marketing, demonstrating how different companies have used these approaches to improve their understanding of consumers and optimize their marketing strategies.

One notable example is a large e-commerce

company that used predictive analytics to personalize product recommendations for its customers. By analyzing historical purchase data, browsing preferences, and user interactions with products, the company was able to create machine learning algorithms to predict which products would be most interesting to each customer. This personalized approach not only increased conversion rates but also improved customers' shopping experience, thereby strengthening their brand loyalty.

In the financial services industry, one bank implemented behavioral analytics techniques to detect and prevent fraud. By analyzing customer transaction patterns and browsing behaviors, the bank was able to identify suspicious activities that deviated from normal customer behaviors. This proactive fraud detection helped the bank protect its customers and reduce financial losses due to fraudulent activities.

Another case study involves a telecommunications company that used predictive analytics to reduce churn. By analyzing customer data, such as service usage, customer service interactions, and reasons for complaints, the company was able to identify customers at risk of churn. By targeting these customers with personalized offers and proactive interventions, the company was able to improve customer satisfaction and significantly reduce its churn rate.

In the health field, a pharmaceutical company used behavioral analysis to optimize its awareness campaigns. By analyzing data on online search habits and social media interactions, the company was able to identify patient groups most likely to be interested in its medications. Targeted campaigns not only improved the effectiveness of marketing efforts, but also helped patients access the information and treatments they needed more quickly.

Finally, an entertainment company used predictive analytics to optimize its content programming. By analyzing viewing data, user preferences and market trends, the company was able to predict which content genres would be most popular and plan its programming accordingly. This data-driven strategy has allowed the company to attract and retain a wider audience, thereby increasing its success and profitability.

These case studies show how predictive and behavioral analytics can be applied across various industries to improve consumer understanding, optimize marketing strategies, and improve business results. By harnessing the power of data, businesses can make more informed decisions, deliver personalized customer experiences, and stay competitive in an ever-changing business environment.

4.3 Data Analysis and Interpretation Tools

4.3.1 Overview of analysis tools

In 2024, the range of data analysis and interpretation tools available for digital marketing is wider and more sophisticated than ever. These tools play a crucial role in helping businesses transform the vast amounts of data collected into actionable and strategic insights. They vary in complexity and functionality, from basic data analysis solutions to advanced platforms integrating artificial intelligence and machine learning.

Web analysis tools, such as Google Analytics, remain essential for monitoring and analyzing web traffic. They provide detailed information about user behavior on websites, including pages visited, session duration, bounce rates, and conversion paths. These tools are essential for understanding how users interact with a website and for identifying optimization opportunities to improve user experience and increase conversions.

For social media analytics, tools like Hootsuite, Sprout Social, and Buffer offer functionality for tracking and analyzing performance across various social media platforms. These tools allow businesses to monitor brand mentions, analyze user engagement, track follower growth, and measure the effectiveness of social media campaigns. They are crucial for adjusting content and engagement strategies on social media.

Advanced data analytics platforms, such as Tableau, Qlik, and Microsoft Power BI, enable deeper data visualization and analysis. These tools provide powerful data visualization capabilities, allowing businesses to create interactive dashboards and custom reports. They are particularly useful for multidimensional analyzes and obtaining insights from large amounts of data.

The integration of artificial intelligence and machine learning into analytics tools has also opened up new possibilities. Platforms like IBM Watson and Salesforce Einstein provide predictive analytics and natural language processing capabilities, allowing businesses to predict future trends, analyze customer sentiment, and automate complex analytics tasks. These tools are particularly valuable for businesses looking to harness the potential of Big Data and gain deeper, more nuanced insights.

Finally, customer relationship management (CRM) tools with analytics capabilities, like Salesforce or HubSpot, allow businesses to combine sales, marketing, and customer service data to get a comprehensive view of customer interactions. clients. These systems help track the customer journey, segment customers, and personalize interactions, playing a key role in improving customer experience and increasing brand loyalty. In conclusion, the overview of analytics tools in 2024 shows a rich and diverse landscape, providing businesses with a multitude of options for analyzing and interpreting data. The selection and effective use of these tools is essential for businesses looking to get the most out of their data and make informed marketing decisions in an ever-changing business environment.

4.3.2 Data interpretation

In 2024, data interpretation in digital marketing has become an essential skill, enabling businesses to transform massive volumes of raw data into strategic, actionable insights. Data interpretation goes beyond simple collection and analysis; it involves understanding context, inferring meanings, and drawing relevant conclusions that can guide marketing decisions.

Effective data interpretation starts with a clear understanding of business and marketing objectives. Before diving into analysis, it is crucial to define what the business is seeking to understand or achieve. This may include identifying new market segments, improving customer experience, increasing conversion rates, or understanding the reasons for declining sales. Having clear objectives helps guide the analysis and ensure that the insights obtained are relevant and useful.

Once the objectives are defined, the next step is to analyze the data taking into account the specific context of the company and the market. This involves looking beyond the numbers and understanding the underlying factors that can influence results. For example, a decline in sales in a specific region could be due to external factors such as economic changes or competitive trends, rather than internal issues.

Interpretation of data also requires a critical and analytical approach. Businesses must be able to distinguish correlation from causation and be aware of potential biases in data. For example, an increase in website traffic does not necessarily mean an increase in product interest; it could also be the result of seasonal factors or recent marketing campaigns.

Using data visualizations is a powerful tool in data interpretation. Graphs, dashboards, and heat maps can help present data in a way that trends, patterns, and anomalies are easily identifiable. Effective visualization makes data more accessible and understandable, facilitating data-driven decision-making.

Finally, the interpretation of the data must translate into concrete actions. Insights obtained from data should be used to inform marketing strategies, to make changes to products or services, or to improve business processes. For example, if the analysis reveals that certain products are particularly popular with a customer segment, the company may choose to focus its marketing efforts on that segment or expand its product line in that category.

In conclusion, data interpretation in 2024 is a complex process that requires a clear understanding of objectives, contextual analysis, critical thinking, effective data visualization and translation of insights into actions. Businesses that master the art of data interpretation are better equipped to navigate the dynamic digital marketing landscape, effectively meet their customers' needs, and remain competitive in an ever-changing business environment.

4.3.3 Data visualization

In 2024, data visualization has become a crucial part of digital marketing, playing a vital role in how businesses understand and communicate insights from their analytics. Data visualization transforms complex sets of data into clear, understandable graphical representations, making interpretation and decision-making easier.

Data visualization helps present complex information in an intuitive and engaging way. Graphs, charts, heat maps, and infographics transform raw numbers into easily digestible visuals. For example, an interactive dashboard can display the performance of a marketing campaign through a series of graphs, allowing marketers to quickly assess which aspects of the campaign are working well and which require adjustment.

One of the main benefits of data visualization is its ability to reveal trends and patterns that might go unnoticed in tables of raw data. For example, a visualization can highlight seasonal trends in consumer purchasing behaviors or show correlations between certain marketing activities and spikes in sales. These insights can help businesses optimize their marketing strategies and target their efforts more effectively.

Data visualization is also essential for communicating complex insights to stakeholders who may not have expertise in data analysis. Clear, attractive visuals can make data more accessible to cross-functional teams, management, or even external customers. By presenting data in an understandable way, businesses can facilitate more productive discussions and informed decision-making.

Modern data visualization tools offer considerable flexibility and interactivity. Platforms like Tableau, Microsoft Power BI, and Qlik Sense allow users to create custom visualizations tailored to their specific needs. These tools offer features such as interactive filtering, real-time analytics, and the ability to explore data at different levels of granularity.

Additionally, data visualization plays an important role in detecting anomalies and potential problems. By visualizing data, businesses can quickly identify deviations from normal trends, which may be a sign of underlying problems in marketing strategies or business operations. This early detection allows companies to take corrective action before these problems become more serious.

In conclusion, data visualization in 2024 is an indispensable aspect of data analysis in digital marketing. It not only simplifies and clarifies the interpretation of data, but also effectively communicates complex insights, reveals important trends and patterns, and facilitates data-driven decision making. In a world where data is increasingly abundant and complex, effective data visualization is essential to transform insights into strategic actions.

4.3.4 Integration of insights into strategy

In 2024, integrating insights from data analysis into marketing strategy has become an essential practice for businesses looking to stay competitive in an ever-changing digital environment. This integration allows businesses to make informed decisions, optimize their campaigns and respond more effectively to consumer needs and expectations.

Integrating insights into marketing strategy starts with a deep understanding of the data collected and analyzed. Insights can reveal information about consumer preferences, marketing channel effectiveness, market trends, and purchasing behaviors. For these insights to be useful, they must be relevant, reliable and actionable. This not only involves having advanced analysis tools, but also a team capable of correctly interpreting the data.

Once the insights are obtained, the next step is to integrate them into the planning and execution of marketing strategies. This may involve adjusting advertising campaigns, personalizing offers for different customer segments, or modifying products and services to better meet market needs. For example, if data reveals high demand for a certain type of product, the company can increase production of that product or develop additional variants.

Integrating insights into marketing strategy also requires a flexible and responsive approach. The market and consumer behaviors are changing rapidly, and businesses must be prepared to adjust their strategies based on new information. This may involve testing different approaches, measuring results, and making quick adjustments to optimize performance.

Cross-functional collaboration is essential to effectively integrating insights into marketing strategy. Marketing, sales, product, and customer service teams must work together to ensure insights are shared and used consistently across the organization. This collaboration ensures that all decisions are made with a complete view of the customer and market in mind.

Finally, integrating insights into marketing strategy should be an ongoing process. Companies must establish mechanisms to continually monitor performance, collect new data, and adjust their strategies accordingly. This involves not only tracking KPIs and performance metrics, but also staying tuned to changes in consumer preferences and market dynamics.

In conclusion, integrating insights from data analysis into marketing strategy in 2024 is a crucial aspect for business success. By using data to inform decisions, remaining flexible and responsive, and fostering cross-functional collaboration, businesses can create more targeted, personalized, and effective marketing strategies, strengthening their market position and improving the customer experience.

CONCLUSION

"Constantly re-evaluating your beliefs is essential for innovation."

Elon Musk

Summary of key trends

In conclusion, the year 2024 will be marked by several key trends in the field of digital marketing, reflecting the rapid evolution of technologies and consumer behaviors. These trends have shaped the way businesses approach marketing and interact with their audiences.

First, the increased importance of Big Data in digital marketing is undeniable. Businesses have adopted sophisticated strategies to collect, analyze and use large amounts of data to better understand and meet the needs of their customers. The analysis of this data has enabled further personalization of marketing campaigns, more precise market segmentation and a better understanding of the customer journey.

Second, predictive and behavioral analytics have

taken center stage, allowing businesses to not only understand past and present consumer actions, but also predict future trends. This approach has allowed businesses to be more proactive in their marketing strategies, anticipating customer needs and tailoring their offerings accordingly.

Blockchain technology has also emerged as a powerful tool for increasing transparency and security in digital marketing. Its application in product traceability, loyalty program management and digital advertising has helped build consumer trust and improve the effectiveness of marketing campaigns.

Additionally, the integration of augmented reality (AR) and virtual reality (VR) technologies has opened new avenues for creating immersive and interactive customer experiences. These technologies have enabled brands to stand out by offering unique and memorable experiences, thereby strengthening customer engagement and loyalty.

The use of data analysis and visualization tools played a crucial role in interpreting and communicating insights. These tools have enabled businesses to transform complex data into understandable and actionable insights, facilitating data-driven decision-making.

Finally, integrating insights into marketing strategy has been essential for business success. By using data to inform decisions, businesses have been able to create more targeted, personalized and effective marketing strategies.

These key 2024 trends demonstrate the growing importance of data analytics, technology and personalization in digital marketing. Companies that have adopted and integrated these trends into their marketing strategies have not only improved their relationship with customers, but also strengthened their position in an increasingly competitive market.

Tips for Staying Up to Date

To stay up to date in the ever-changing field of digital marketing in 2024, it is essential for professionals and businesses to follow a proactive and informed approach. Here are some key tips for staying at the forefront of this dynamic industry.

First of all, continuing education is crucial. The digital marketing landscape is rapidly evolving with the introduction of new technologies and strategies. Professionals must therefore engage in continuous learning to stay informed of the latest trends, tools and best practices. This may involve attending webinars, conferences, workshops, or taking online courses on relevant topics such as data analysis, artificial intelligence in marketing, or the latest trends in social media .

Second, it is important to practice active technological and market monitoring. This means following industry publications, blogs, podcasts and influencers who share insights on the latest developments in digital marketing. Subscribing to relevant newsletters, following thought leaders on social media, and participating in professional online groups can provide valuable information and up-to-date perspectives.

Collaboration and networking also play an important role. Connecting with peers, industry experts and professionals from other sectors can offer new ideas and perspectives. Participating in industry events, online forums and discussion groups can help stay connected with current trends and share experiences and knowledge.

Experimenting with new technologies and strategies is also essential. Businesses must be willing to test and implement new approaches into their marketing strategies. This may involve experimenting with augmented reality campaigns, adopting predictive analytics tools, or exploring new social media channels. Experimentation not only allows you to understand what works best, but also to innovate and stand out in a competitive market.

Finally, it is crucial to remain customer-centric. Despite the rapid evolution of technologies and tools, the main objective of digital marketing remains to meet the needs and expectations of customers. Businesses must therefore continue to listen to their customers, collect feedback and adapt their strategies to deliver exceptional customer experiences.

In summary, to stay up to date in digital marketing

in 2024, it is essential to engage in continuous learning, practice active monitoring, collaborate and network with industry professionals, experiment with new technologies and strategies, and to remain customer-centric. By adopting these approaches, professionals and businesses can not only keep pace with rapid changes, but also take advantage of emerging opportunities in this dynamic field.

Future vision of digital marketing

As we envision the future of digital marketing beyond 2024, several trends and developments promise to significantly shape the landscape of this industry. The continued convergence of technology, data and creativity has the potential to create new opportunities and challenges for marketers.

One of the most significant trends is the continued rise of artificial intelligence (AI) and machine learning. These technologies are expected to become even more sophisticated, enabling even greater personalization and automation in marketing campaigns. AI could help create hyper-personalized customer experiences, where messages and offers are adapted in real time based on each individual's behavior and preferences. Additionally, AI could play a crucial role in predictive analytics, helping businesses anticipate customer needs before they even arise.

Augmented reality (AR) and virtual reality (VR) are also expected to continue to transform the customer experience. These technologies could become mainstream tools for consumer engagement, providing immersive and interactive experiences that go beyond traditional screens. Brands could use AR and VR to deliver virtual shopping experiences, interactive product demonstrations, or even to create fully immersive brand worlds.

Privacy and data ethics will remain major areas of concern. With increased data collection, businesses will need to navigate an ever-changing regulatory landscape while maintaining consumer trust. Brands that successfully balance innovation with data responsibility will earn the trust and loyalty of their customers.

The future of digital marketing will also see deeper integration between online and offline channels. Omnichannel marketing, which provides a seamless and consistent customer experience across all channels, will become the norm. Businesses will use integrated data to deliver seamless experiences, whether customers interact online, through mobile apps, or in-store.

Finally, continued innovation in communication channels and social media platforms will open new avenues for consumer engagement. New platforms could emerge, offering unique and innovative ways to connect brands with their audiences. Businesses will need to remain agile and ready to explore these new channels to stay relevant to their audiences.

In summary, the future vision of digital marketing is characterized by rapid technological innovation, increased personalization, renewed attention to privacy and ethics, omnichannel integration and the emergence of new communication channels. Companies that embrace these developments and adapt their strategies accordingly will be well positioned to succeed in this dynamic and ever-changing landscape.

ANNEXES

Glossary of Technical Terms

In the ever-changing field of digital marketing, being familiar with technical jargon is essential. Here is a glossary of technical terms frequently used in digital marketing in 2024:

1. **Big Data** : A collection of extremely large and complex data that cannot be processed effectively with traditional data processing methods. Big Data is crucial for analyzing trends and behaviors in digital marketing.

2. **Blockchain** : Distributed ledger technology that allows data to be stored securely and transparently. In marketing, it is used for product traceability, loyalty program management, and digital advertising.

3. **Chatbot** : A computer program that uses AI to simulate a conversation with human users, often used in customer service and automated interactions on

websites and applications.

4. **Content Marketing** : Marketing strategy focused on creating and distributing relevant and valuable content to attract and engage a target audience.

5. **Conversion Rate Optimization (CRO)** : The process of optimizing websites and landing pages to increase the percentage of visitors who take the desired action.

6. **Customer Relationship Management (CRM)** : System used to manage customer interactions and relationships, centralizing customer, sales and service information.

7. **Data Mining** : The process of analyzing large amounts of data to discover hidden patterns and relationships.

8. **Inbound Marketing** : Marketing approach that aims to attract customers by creating useful content and tailored experiences.

9. **Machine Learning** : A branch of artificial intelligence that allows systems to learn and improve from experience without being explicitly programmed.

10. **Programmatic Advertising** : Using automated software to purchase and optimize advertising placements in real time.

11. **Search Engine Optimization (SEO)** : The process of optimizing a website to improve its ranking in search engine results.
12. **Social Media Marketing** : Using social media platforms to promote a product or service.
13. **User Experience (UX)** : All interactions and experiences that a user has with a digital product or service.
14. **Virtual Reality (VR)** : Technology that creates a simulated environment, allowing users to immerse and interact in a virtual world.
15. **Web Analytics** : Process of collecting, analyzing and reporting web traffic data to understand and optimize web usage.

This glossary provides a foundation for understanding technical terms commonly used in digital marketing, allowing professionals and students to better navigate this complex and ever-changing field.

In-Depth Case Studies

1. E-Commerce Revolution at Luxomoda: Integration of AI for a Personalized Customer Experience

Context: Luxomoda, a luxury brand, faced an increasingly competitive market and high customer expectations for personalization. To remain competitive and improve customer experience, Luxomoda has decided to integrate artificial intelligence (AI) into its e-commerce platform.

Objective: Luxomoda's main objective was to create a highly personalized online shopping experience for each customer, using AI to analyze customer data and provide tailored product recommendations, style suggestions and a improved customer service.

Implementation: Luxomoda collaborated with a leading technology company to integrate advanced AI algorithms into its website and mobile app. These algorithms were designed to learn about customers' purchasing behaviors, preferences, and interactions with the site.

1. **Personalized Recommendations:** AI analyzed purchase histories, site clicks and style preferences to recommend specific products to each customer. This included suggestions for completing a purchase or discovering new items that fit the customer's style.

2. **Virtual Style Assistant:** Luxomoda has introduced an AI-powered chatbot, acting as a personal style assistant, offering fashion advice and answering

customer questions in real time.

3. **Predictive Analytics:** AI has also been used to predict fashion trends and customer preferences, allowing Luxomoda to stock items likely to be a big hit.

Results: AI integration has transformed the shopping experience at Luxomoda:

- **Increased Sales:** Personalized recommendations led to a significant increase in conversion rates and average order value.

- **Improved Customer Engagement:** The virtual style assistant has improved customer engagement, providing an interactive and personalized shopping experience.

- **Optimized Inventory Management:** Predictive analysis has enabled Luxomoda to better manage its inventory, reducing surpluses and stock-outs.

- **Increased Customer Satisfaction:** Customer feedback has been extremely positive, with a notable increase in customer satisfaction and brand loyalty.

Conclusion: The Luxomoda case study demonstrates the powerful impact of AI in personalizing the online shopping experience. By adopting innovative technologies, Luxomoda has not only improved its business performance but also set a new standard in customer experience for the luxury sector.

2. Biotec Pharma Omnichannel Strategy: Using Data Science to Transform the Customer Journey in the Pharmaceutical Sector

Context: Biotec Pharma, a leading company in the pharmaceutical sector, identified the need to improve its customers' experience by integrating an omnichannel strategy. Faced with an increasingly digitalized market and customers looking for fluid and personalized interactions, Biotec Pharma decided to use data science to transform its customer journey.

Objective: Biotec Pharma's goal was to create a consistent and personalized customer experience across all channels - online, mobile, and in-store - using data to understand and anticipate customer needs.

Implementation: To achieve this objective, Biotec Pharma has implemented several key initiatives:

1. **Data Integration:** Biotec Pharma has consolidated customer data from various sources, including online interactions, in-store purchases, and responses to marketing campaigns. The goal was to create a 360-degree view of each customer.

2. **Predictive Analytics:** Using advanced data science techniques, the company

analyzed this data to identify behavioral patterns, predict customer needs and personalize interactions.

3. **Omnichannel Personalization:** Based on these analyses, Biotec Pharma personalized the customer experience across all channels. This included personalized product recommendations on the website, relevant mobile notifications and personalized in-store customer service.

4. **Customer Relationship Management (CRM) Platform:** An advanced CRM platform has been implemented to manage customer interactions in a consistent and integrated manner across all channels.

Results: Biotec Pharma's omnichannel strategy has led to several positive results:

- **Improved Customer Experience:** Customers benefited from a smoother and more personalized experience, increasing their satisfaction and brand loyalty.

- **Increased Sales:** Data-driven personalization has led to increased sales, both online and in-store.

- **Better Customer Understanding:** Data analysis has enabled Biotec Pharma to better understand the needs and preferences of its customers, thereby improving decision-making in product development and marketing.

- **Operational Efficiency:** Data integration across channels has improved operational efficiency, reducing duplication and optimizing marketing resources.

Conclusion: The Biotec Pharma case study illustrates the importance of an integrated omnichannel strategy in the pharmaceutical sector. By harnessing the power of data science, Biotec Pharma has not only improved customer experience but also strengthened its position in the market. This data-centric, customer-first approach is a model for other companies looking to transform their customer journey in an increasingly digitalized business environment.

3. Augmented Reality Innovation at HomeSpace: Redefining the Online Furniture Shopping Experience

Background: HomeSpace, an online furniture sales company, recognized the opportunity to improve its customers' shopping experience by integrating augmented reality (AR) into its sales process. Faced with the difficulty for customers to visualize furniture in their own space, HomeSpace sought to use AR to offer an innovative solution.

Objective: The main objective of HomeSpace

was to provide an immersive and interactive shopping experience that allows customers to view products in their own environment before making a purchase. This aimed to reduce customer uncertainty, increase satisfaction and reduce product returns.

Implementation: To achieve this goal, HomeSpace has developed and integrated several key AR features:

1. **AR App:** HomeSpace launched a mobile app allowing customers to virtually visualize the furniture in their space. Using the camera on their smartphone or tablet, customers could place a 3D piece of furniture in their room and view it from different angles and in different locations.

2. **Real-Time Customization:** The app also allowed customers to personalize products in real time, changing colors, textures and dimensions to see how different options would fit into their space.

3. **E-commerce integration:** The application was integrated with HomeSpace's e-commerce site, allowing customers to directly place an order after viewing a product in AR.

4. **Guides and Tutorials:** HomeSpace has

provided guides and tutorials to help customers use the AR application, ensuring a smooth user experience.

Results: The introduction of AR at HomeSpace led to several positive results:

- **Increased Customer Engagement:** The immersive experience increased customer engagement, encouraging them to explore more products and spend more time on the app.

- **Reduced Returns:** The ability to view products in their own space has reduced customer uncertainty, leading to a significant decrease in returns.

- **Increased Sales:** The improved shopping experience led to increased sales as customers felt more confident in their product choices.

- **Improved Customer Satisfaction:** Positive customer feedback indicated a significant improvement in customer satisfaction, strengthening brand loyalty.

Conclusion: The HomeSpace case study demonstrates the transformative impact of augmented reality in the furniture e-commerce industry. By adopting this innovative technology, HomeSpace has not only improved the online shopping experience, but also set a new standard in the industry, showing how AR can be used to bridge the gap between online shopping experiences and in store.

4. GreenEarth Viral Campaign: Using Social Media for Impactful Environmental Awareness

Background: GreenEarth, a nonprofit organization dedicated to environmental awareness, recognized the potential of social media to reach a broad audience and engage the community on critical environmental issues. In the face of the climate emergency and growing public indifference, GreenEarth launched a viral social media campaign to raise awareness and incite action.

Goal: GreenEarth's goal was to create a viral social media campaign that raises awareness of the environmental emergency, encourages content sharing, and inspires individuals and communities to take concrete action to protect the environment.

Implementation: To achieve this objective, GreenEarth has implemented several key initiatives:

1. **Engaging and Educational Content:** GreenEarth has created a series of informative and visually appealing videos, infographics and blog posts, highlighting various environmental issues and offering practical solutions.

2. **Hashtags and Challenges:** The

organization launched campaign-specific hashtags and challenges on social media, encouraging users to share their own actions for the environment, creating a community movement.

3. **Collaboration with Influencers:** GreenEarth collaborated with influencers and celebrities committed to environmental causes to expand the campaign's reach and reach a wider audience.

4. **Interactivity and Engagement:** The campaign was designed to be highly interactive, with polls, live Q&As, and discussion forums to engage the audience and encourage active participation.

Results: GreenEarth's viral campaign had a significant impact:

- **Extensive Reach:** The campaign reached millions of people around the world, far exceeding initial expectations in terms of reach and engagement.

- **Community Engagement:** Challenges and hashtags encouraged active participation, with thousands of people sharing their environmental actions, creating an engaged online community.

- **Increased Awareness:** The campaign was successful in raising awareness on important environmental issues, with an increasing number of people discussing and sharing information on these topics.

- **Real Impact:** Beyond online awareness, the campaign led to concrete actions, such as community clean-up initiatives, waste reduction commitments and donations to environmental causes.

Conclusion: The GreenEarth case study illustrates the power of social media to run impactful environmental awareness campaigns. By combining engaging content, strategic use of social media, and collaboration with influencers, GreenEarth has not only raised awareness of crucial environmental issues, but also mobilized a global community to take action. This campaign serves as a model for other organizations seeking to use social media for positive social and environmental impact.

5. BankSecure Digital Transformation: Securing Financial Transactions with Blockchain

Background: BankSecure, a leading bank in the financial sector, has identified a growing need to strengthen the security and transparency of its financial transactions in the face of an increase in cyberattacks and fraud. To respond to this challenge, BankSecure decided to adopt blockchain technology, recognized for its robustness in terms of security and traceability of transactions.

Objective: BankSecure's main objective was to integrate blockchain into its existing infrastructure to secure financial transactions, reduce fraud risks and improve customer trust in digital banking services.

Implementation: To achieve this objective, BankSecure implemented several key initiatives:

1. **Blockchain Infrastructure:** BankSecure has developed a customized blockchain infrastructure, adapted to the specific needs of the banking sector. This infrastructure made it possible to record all transactions on a distributed, secure and immutable ledger.

2. **Systems Integration:** Blockchain has been integrated with the bank's existing systems, including online payment platforms and mobile applications, to ensure a smooth transition and maintain continuity of services.

3. **Training and Awareness:** BankSecure has invested in blockchain training for its staff and has run awareness campaigns for its customers, explaining the benefits of the new technology in terms of

security and reliability.

4. **Testing and Compliance:** Before full deployment, the blockchain solution was rigorously tested to ensure compliance with financial regulations and compatibility with banking security standards.

Results: BankSecure's blockchain integration led to several positive results:

- **Strengthening Security:** Blockchain has significantly strengthened the security of transactions, reducing incidents of fraud and processing errors.

- **Increased Transparency:** The traceability and immutability of transactions on the blockchain have improved transparency, strengthening customer confidence in the bank's services.

- **Operational Efficiency:** Blockchain has simplified and accelerated the transaction verification process, improving the operational efficiency of the bank.

- **Regulatory Compliance:** The blockchain solution has helped BankSecure more easily comply with financial regulations regarding reporting and auditing.

Conclusion: The BankSecure case study demonstrates the effectiveness of blockchain in the digital transformation of the banking sector. By adopting this technology, BankSecure has not only improved the security and transparency of its transactions, but has also positioned the bank as an innovative leader in the adoption of advanced technological solutions. This initiative serves as a model for other financial institutions seeking to enhance security and trust in the digital age.

6. SportsVirtu's Winning Bet: Fan Engagement with Immersive Virtual Reality Experiences

Context: SportsVirtu, a company specializing in virtual sports experiences, has identified a unique opportunity to transform fan engagement in the world of sports. With the growing popularity of virtual reality (VR), SportsVirtu envisioned creating immersive experiences to bring fans closer to their favorite teams and athletes in a way never before seen.

Objective: SportsVirtu's objective was to develop a VR platform offering immersive and interactive sports experiences, allowing fans to experience matches and sporting events as if they were there, while offering unique interactive and social features.

Implementation: To achieve this ambitious goal, SportsVirtu has launched several key initiatives:

1. **VR Platform Development:** SportsVirtu has developed an advanced VR platform, allowing users to experience matches in

real time with a 360-degree view from different locations in the stadium.

2. **Partnerships with Sports Teams and Leagues:** To deliver authentic and engaging content, SportsVirtu has partnered with several sports teams and leagues, allowing them to stream live matches on the platform.

3. **Interactive Features:** The platform offered interactive features, such as selection of different viewing angles, access to real-time statistics, and communication options with other fans.

4. **Immersive Non-Match Experiences:** In addition to live matches, SportsVirtu has created immersive non-match experiences, such as virtual stadium tours, meetings with athletes in VR, and interactive games.

Results: The SportsVirtu initiative had a significant impact on fan engagement:

- **Increased Fan Engagement:** The platform attracted a growing number of fans, providing an immersive and interactive experience that strengthened their connection with their favorite teams and athletes.

- **New Revenue:** The platform has opened up new revenue streams, including subscriptions, in-app advertising, and exclusive partnerships with teams and leagues.

- **Enhanced Fan Experience:** Fans benefited from an enriched sports experience, with customization and interaction options that were not possible with traditional viewing methods.
- **Industry Recognition:** SportsVirtu has been recognized as an innovator in sports, setting new standards for fan engagement in the digital age.

Conclusion: The SportsVirtu case study illustrates the revolutionary potential of VR in sports fan engagement. By leveraging this technology, SportsVirtu has not only enhanced the fan experience, but also paved the way for new business opportunities and a new era of interaction between fans and the world of sports.

7. HealthFirst Content Strategy: Education and Customer Engagement in the Healthcare Sector

Context: HealthFirst, a leading healthcare company, recognized the need to improve customer education and engagement in the face of an increasingly health-conscious public hungry for trusted information. To meet this growing demand, HealthFirst decided to implement a robust and informative content strategy.

Objective: HealthFirst's goal was to develop and implement a content strategy that educates customers on various health topics, promotes healthy behaviors, and builds engagement and brand loyalty.

Implementation: To achieve this goal, HealthFirst launched several key initiatives:

1. **Educational Content Creation:** HealthFirst has developed a series of educational content, including blog posts, videos, infographics and podcasts, covering a wide range of health topics, from disease prevention to nutrition and wellness. -be mental.

2. **Online Platform and Mobile Application:** This content has been made easily accessible via a dedicated online platform and mobile application, allowing customers to find reliable and practical information at any time.

3. **Interactive Programs:** HealthFirst has introduced interactive programs, such as wellness challenges and live webinars with health experts, to encourage active customer engagement.

4. **Content Personalization:** Using customer data, HealthFirst personalized content recommendations to meet each

user's specific needs and interests.

5. **Collaboration with Experts:** To ensure content accuracy and reliability, HealthFirst collaborated with healthcare professionals and industry experts to create and review all educational materials.

Results: HealthFirst's content strategy led to several positive results:

- **Improved Customer Engagement:** Educational and interactive content significantly increased customer engagement, with a notable increase in time spent on the platform and interaction with content.

- **Strengthening Brand Loyalty:** By providing reliable and useful information, HealthFirst has strengthened customer trust and loyalty towards the brand.

- **Increased Health Awareness:** The strategy has contributed to greater awareness and education of customers on important health issues, encouraging healthier lifestyle choices.

- **Positive ROI:** The content strategy also led to a positive ROI, with increased health program enrollment and increased usage of HealthFirst services.

Conclusion: The HealthFirst case study demonstrates the importance of an educational and engaging content strategy in the healthcare industry. By providing trusted information and encouraging active engagement, HealthFirst has not only improved the health and well-being of its customers, but also strengthened its position as a trusted brand and leader in healthcare.

8. FashionFlare Influencer Marketing Campaign: Measuring Impact and ROI in Luxury

Context: FashionFlare, a recognized luxury brand, was looking to strengthen its presence and brand image in a highly competitive market. To achieve this goal, FashionFlare launched an influencer marketing campaign, partnering with leading fashion influencers to reach a wider, more engaged audience.

Objective: FashionFlare's main objective was to measure the impact and return on investment (ROI) of its influencer marketing campaign, assessing not only the increase in brand awareness, but also the influence on sales and customer engagement.

Implementation: To carry out this campaign, FashionFlare adopted a strategic and measurable approach:

1. **Selection of Influencers:** FashionFlare carefully selected influencers whose style and audience matched FashionFlare's brand image and values. This selection included influencers with large

followings and high engagement rates.

2. **Consistent Brand Content:** Influencers created personalized content that highlighted FashionFlare's products while staying true to their own unique style. This included social media posts, blogs, and videos.

3. **Tracking and Analytics:** FashionFlare used advanced analytics tools to track each influencer's performance, including engagement, reach, and traffic driven to FashionFlare's website.

4. **Promo Codes and Tracking Links:** Unique promo codes and tracking links were provided to influencers to directly measure sales and conversions resulting from the campaign.

5. **Feedback and Interaction:** FashionFlare encouraged influencers to interact with their audience, collecting valuable feedback and building engagement with the brand.

Results: FashionFlare's influencer marketing campaign produced significant results:

- **Increased Brand Awareness:** The campaign significantly increased awareness of FashionFlare, attracting a new audience and strengthening its social media presence.

- **Sales Growth:** Promo codes and tracking

links showed a noticeable increase in sales directly attributable to the campaign.

- **Increased Engagement:** Content created by influencers generated high engagement, with meaningful interactions between consumers and the brand.
- **Positive ROI:** Data analysis showed a positive return on investment, with the profits generated by the campaign far exceeding the initial costs.

Conclusion: The FashionFlare case study illustrates the effectiveness of influencer marketing in the luxury sector. By taking a strategic approach and carefully measuring the impact of the campaign, FashionFlare not only improved its brand awareness, but also generated significant customer engagement and sales growth. This campaign serves as a model for other luxury brands looking to harness the power of influencer marketing to reach new heights.

9. QuickServe Mobile Marketing Initiative: Reinventing Fast Food with Innovative Applications

Background: QuickServe, a popular fast food chain, has seen a steady shift in consumer habits, with an increase in demand for faster, more convenient ordering and delivery options. To meet these expectations, QuickServe decided to launch a mobile marketing initiative, focused on the development of innovative mobile applications.

Goal: QuickServe's goal was to create an enhanced mobile user experience that makes ordering, meal customization, and delivery easier, while using the app as a marketing tool to build customer loyalty and increase sales.

Implementation: To achieve this goal, QuickServe has implemented several key strategies:

1. **Development of an Intuitive Mobile Application:** QuickServe has developed a user-friendly mobile application, offering easy navigation, quick ordering, and meal customization options. The app also integrated a secure payment system for a hassle-free ordering experience.

2. **Integrated Loyalty Program:** The app included a loyalty program, offering personalized rewards and promotions based on users' preferences and ordering habits.

3. **Augmented Reality Features:** QuickServe has innovated by integrating augmented reality (AR) features into its app, allowing customers to view meals before ordering and participate in interactive games to earn rewards.

4. **Push Notifications and Targeted Marketing:** The app used push

notifications to inform customers of special offers, new products, and local events, thereby increasing engagement and repeat visits.

5. **User Data Analysis:** QuickServe collected and analyzed user data to understand customer preferences and tailor its offers and marketing accordingly.

Results: QuickServe's mobile marketing initiative led to several positive results:

- **Increased Sales:** The app has driven a significant increase in online orders and overall sales, providing a convenient and quick ordering experience.
- **Increased Customer Engagement:** The loyalty program and push notifications increased customer engagement, leading to increased order frequency and brand loyalty.
- **Improved Customer Experience:** AR features and personalization options have improved the customer experience, making ordering more interactive and enjoyable.
- **Valuable Customer Insights:** Analyzing user data provided QuickServe with valuable insights to optimize its menus, promotional offers and marketing strategies.

Conclusion: The QuickServe case study demonstrates the significant impact of a well-designed mobile application in the fast food industry. By combining an intuitive user experience with innovative mobile marketing strategies, QuickServe has not only improved the ordering experience for its customers, but also seen a notable increase in customer engagement and sales. This initiative serves as a model for other companies in the industry looking to leverage mobile technologies to reinvent the customer experience.

10. Customer Loyalty Project at AutoElite: Using Blockchain-Based Loyalty Programs to Improve Retention

Context: AutoElite, a leading automobile manufacturer, has seen declining customer loyalty in an increasingly competitive market. To reverse this trend, AutoElite decided to innovate by launching a loyalty program based on blockchain technology, aiming to offer a more transparent, secure and rewarding customer experience.

Goal: AutoElite's goal was to develop a loyalty program that not only rewards customers for their loyalty, but also uses the benefits of blockchain to improve security, transparency and personalization of rewards.

Implementation: To achieve this objective, AutoElite has implemented several key initiatives:

1. **Development of a Blockchain Platform:**

AutoElite has developed a blockchain-based loyalty platform, enabling secure and transparent recording of customer transactions and interactions.

2. **Innovative Rewards System:** The program offered rewards in the form of blockchain tokens, which could be exchanged for services, accessories, or even discounts on vehicles. These tokens could also be accumulated or exchanged with other members of the program.

3. **Personalization of Offers:** Using customer data collected through the platform, AutoElite personalized offers and rewards based on each customer's preferences and purchasing behavior.

4. **Integrated Mobile Application:** A mobile application has been developed to allow customers to easily track their tokens, discover new offers and manage their loyalty account.

5. **Awareness and Training Campaigns:** AutoElite has conducted campaigns to educate customers on the benefits of blockchain and how to use the new loyalty program.

Results: AutoElite's customer loyalty initiative produced significant results:

- **Improved Customer Loyalty:** The program

strengthened customer loyalty, with a notable increase in retention and purchase frequency.

- **Increased Transparency and Security:** Blockchain has improved the transparency and security of loyalty transactions, increasing customer trust in the program.
- **Increased Customer Engagement:** The mobile app and personalized rewards increased customer engagement with the brand.
- **Positive Return on Investment:** The program generated a positive return on investment, with an increase in vehicle sales and associated services.

Conclusion: The AutoElite case study illustrates how the innovative use of blockchain technology in loyalty programs can transform customer engagement and retention in the automotive industry. By providing a more secure, transparent and personalized loyalty experience, AutoElite has not only improved customer satisfaction, but also strengthened its position in the market as a forward-thinking and customer-centric brand.

11. TravelWorld SEO Optimization: Advanced Strategies to Dominate the Online Travel Market

Background: TravelWorld, an online travel agency, faced fierce competition in a saturated market.

To improve its online visibility and attract more customers, TravelWorld decided to implement advanced search engine optimization (SEO) strategies.

Objective: TravelWorld's objective was to strengthen its online presence, improve its search rankings and attract quality traffic to its website, by focusing on innovative and effective SEO strategies.

Implementation: To achieve this goal, TravelWorld adopted several key approaches:

1. **In-Depth Keyword Research:** TravelWorld conducted extensive keyword research to identify the most relevant and searched terms and phrases in the travel industry. This included long-tail keywords specific to certain destinations and travel types.

2. **Content Optimization:** The content of the TravelWorld website has been optimized to include the identified keywords, ensuring that the content remains informative, engaging and useful to users. Travel guides, blog articles and destination descriptions have been regularly updated and expanded.

3. **Improved User Experience:** TravelWorld has improved its site navigation, loading

speed and mobile friendliness to provide a better user experience, a key factor in SEO ranking.

4. **Backlinking Strategy:** A backlinking strategy was implemented, obtaining high quality links from recognized websites in the travel industry and related media.

5. **Local and International SEO:** TravelWorld has optimized its site for local and international SEO, targeting specific markets with content and keywords tailored to each region.

6. **Analysis and Monitoring:** SEO analysis tools were used to track site performance, allowing TravelWorld to adjust its strategy based on market trends and user behaviors.

Results: TravelWorld SEO optimization led to several positive results:

- **Increase in Organic Traffic:** The site saw a significant increase in organic traffic, attracting more visitors interested in travel.

- **Improved Search Engine Rankings:** TravelWorld saw its rankings improve for many strategic keywords, rising to the top of search results for several key terms.

- **Increased Engagement:** Improved user experience and quality of content have increased visitor engagement on the site.

- **Increased Conversion and Sales:** Increased qualified traffic has led to increased travel bookings and sales.

Conclusion: The TravelWorld case study demonstrates the importance of a robust and well-planned SEO strategy in the online travel industry. By adopting innovative approaches and focusing on continuous improvement, TravelWorld has not only improved its online visibility, but also strengthened its position in the competitive travel market, attracting more customers and generating increased revenue.

12. Techtronics Programmatic Advertising Campaign: Automation and Precise Targeting for Maximum Impact

Context: Techtronics, a leading consumer electronics company, was looking to maximize the impact of its advertising campaigns in a crowded digital marketplace. To achieve this goal, Techtronics decided to adopt programmatic advertising, a method of automating the purchasing and placement of advertisements to target specific audiences more effectively.

Objective: Techtronics' goal was to launch a programmatic advertising campaign that not only reaches its target audience accurately, but also optimizes return on investment (ROI) by using data and algorithms to make purchasing decisions of advertising space in real time.

Implementation: To carry out this campaign, Techtronics implemented several key strategies:

1. **Selection of Programmatic Platforms:** Techtronics has chosen programmatic advertising platforms renowned for their ability to effectively target audiences and provide detailed analytics.

2. **Target Audience Definition:** The company defined its target audience based on demographics, interests, purchasing behaviors and online browsing habits.

3. **Creation of Personalized Advertising Content:** Personalized advertisements were created to resonate with the target audience, using messages and visuals tailored to different user segments.

4. **Real-Time Optimization:** The campaign was constantly monitored and adjusted in real time to optimize performance, based on data such as click-through rates, conversions and engagement.

5. **Multi-Channel Data Integration:** Techtronics integrated data from various channels, including social media, websites and mobile apps, for a holistic

view of campaign effectiveness.

6. **Analysis and Reporting:** Detailed reports were generated to assess campaign performance, including ROI, reach, engagement and conversions.

Results: Techtronics' programmatic advertising campaign led to several positive results:

- **Precise Targeting:** The campaign reached the target audience with high precision, increasing the effectiveness of advertisements and reducing wastage of advertising budget.

- **Increased Engagement:** Personalized ads generated significant engagement, with above-average click-through and conversion rates.

- **ROI Optimization:** Real-time optimization allowed the campaign to be adjusted to maximize ROI, allocating budget to the best performing channels and ads.

- **Deep Insights:** Analytics provided valuable insights into audience behavior and preferences, helping Techtronics refine future marketing strategies.

Conclusion: The Techtronics case study illustrates the effectiveness of programmatic advertising in precisely targeting audiences and maximizing ROI. By adopting a data-driven approach and using automation to adjust the campaign in real time, Techtronics not only improved the performance of its ads, but also gained valuable insights to guide its future marketing initiatives.

13. Corporate Social Responsibility Initiative at EcoPure: Ethical Marketing and Community Engagement

Background: EcoPure, a company specializing in eco-friendly cleaning products, has recognized the growing importance of Corporate Social Responsibility (CSR) in the modern business environment. To strengthen its commitment to sustainability and ethics, EcoPure launched a CSR initiative focused on ethical marketing and community engagement.

Objective: EcoPure's objective was to develop and implement ethical marketing strategies that reflect its values of sustainability and social responsibility, while actively engaging with local communities to promote sound environmental practices.

Implementation: To achieve this goal, EcoPure has adopted several key approaches:

1. **Ethical Marketing:** EcoPure reviewed its marketing strategies to ensure they were aligned with its sustainability principles. This included promoting the use of recyclable materials in its packaging and highlighting its efforts to reduce the carbon footprint.

2. **Environmental Awareness Programs:** EcoPure has launched awareness programs to educate consumers on the importance of sustainability and eco-friendly practices in daily life.

3. **Partnerships with Environmental Organizations:** EcoPure has partnered with local and global environmental organizations to support various conservation and sustainability projects.

4. **Community Initiatives:** EcoPure has organized community events, such as neighborhood cleanups and educational workshops, to encourage active participation in environmental protection.

5. **Transparency and Reporting:** EcoPure has implemented reporting mechanisms to share its CSR progress with its stakeholders, thereby strengthening transparency and trust.

Results: EcoPure's CSR initiative led to several positive results:

- **Brand Strengthening:** EcoPure's commitment to sustainability and social responsibility has strengthened its brand image and reputation among consumers.

- **Increased Community Engagement:** Community initiatives have strengthened EcoPure's connections with local communities, generating goodwill and increased support for the brand.

- **Positive Environmental Impact:** Outreach programs and partnerships have had a positive impact on the environment, contributing to more sustainable practices within the community.
- **Customer Loyalty:** EcoPure's transparency and commitment to CSR have strengthened customer loyalty, attracting consumers who value ethics and sustainability.

Conclusion: The EcoPure case study demonstrates the importance and effectiveness of an ethical marketing approach and strong community engagement as part of a CSR initiative. By aligning its business practices with its sustainability values, EcoPure has not only enhanced its brand image and strengthened its relationships with communities, but has also significantly contributed to important environmental causes, demonstrating the vital role that Companies can play a role in promoting a more sustainable future.

14. GourmetDelight Content Marketing Strategy: Creating a Passionate Community Around Food

Context: GourmetDelight, a company specializing in premium food products, was looking to establish a strong and engaging online presence to connect with food lovers. To achieve this goal, GourmetDelight decided to launch a content marketing strategy aimed at creating an online community of food and cooking enthusiasts.

Objective: GourmetDelight's objective was to develop rich and engaging content that not only informs and educates, but also creates a sense of belonging and engagement among food and cooking enthusiasts.

Implementation: To achieve this goal, GourmetDelight adopted several key strategies:

1. **Blog and Articles:** GourmetDelight has launched a dedicated blog, offering a variety of articles ranging from exclusive recipes and chef tips, to stories about ingredient origins and culinary trends.

2. **Videos and Tutorials:** Cooking videos and tutorials have been produced, featuring renowned chefs and food experts, to provide an interactive and visual learning experience.

3. **Social Media:** GourmetDelight has actively used social media to share content, interact with followers, and encourage users to share their own culinary experiences and creations.

4. **Online Events and Webinars:** Online

events, such as webinars and virtual tastings, have been organized to bring the community together and offer exclusive experiences.

5. **Newsletter:** A regular newsletter has been set up to keep the community informed of the latest news, special offers and events.

6. **Partnerships with Influencers:** Partnerships with culinary influencers have been established to expand the reach of content and attract new members to the community.

Results: GourmetDelight's content marketing strategy led to several positive results:

- **Community Growth:** GourmetDelight's online community has grown rapidly, with a significant increase in subscribers and active participants.

- **Increased Engagement:** Interactive and educational content generated high engagement, with comments, shares and interactions increasing across all platforms.

- **Customer Loyalty:** Creating a passionate community has strengthened customer loyalty, with positive feedback on the products and experiences offered by GourmetDelight.

- **Increased Sales:** The content strategy led to an increase in sales, with community members becoming regular customers and brand ambassadors.

Conclusion: The GourmetDelight case study illustrates the effectiveness of a well-designed content marketing strategy in building and engaging an online community. By providing rich, interactive content that resonates with its audience's passions, GourmetDelight has not only strengthened its online presence, but also established a strong and lasting relationship with its customers, demonstrating the power of content in building a loyal and engaged brand community.

Expert Interviews

1. "Navigating the AI Era": Interview with Dr. Sophie Lemaire, Specialist in Artificial Intelligence and Marketing

Background: Artificial intelligence (AI) is revolutionizing many industries, including marketing. To better understand this development, an interview was conducted with Dr. Sophie Lemaire, a recognized specialist in the field of AI applied to marketing.

Interview Objective: The objective was to gather insights on the impact of AI in marketing, associated challenges, and best practices for effectively integrating AI into marketing strategies.

Key Points of the Interview:

1. **Role of AI in Modern Marketing:**
   - Dr. Lemaire explained how AI is transforming marketing, including enabling deeper personalization, predictive analysis of consumer trends, and automation of repetitive tasks.

2. **AI Integration Challenges:**
   - She highlighted challenges in integrating AI, such as the need for quality data, ethical and privacy concerns, and the need for specialized skills to manage AI technologies.

3. **Success Examples of AI in Marketing:**
   - Dr. Lemaire shared case studies where AI has been successfully used to improve customer engagement, optimize advertising campaigns, and increase sales.

4. **Future of AI in Marketing:**
   - She discussed future trends, predicting an increase in the use of AI for dynamic content creation, customer relationship management, and predictive marketing.

5. **Tips for Businesses Adopting AI:**
   - Dr. Lemaire advised businesses to start small, focus on clear goals, and ensure they have the resources to manage and interpret AI-generated data.

6. **Impact of AI on Marketing Skills:**

○ She also discussed the impact of AI on the skills required in marketing, highlighting the importance of understanding data, analytical thinking, and the ability to work collaboratively with technology.

Interview Conclusion: The interview with Dr. Sophie Lemaire offered valuable perspectives on the growing importance of AI in marketing. Its insights highlight how businesses can navigate this new era, leveraging AI to improve their marketing strategies while remaining attentive to ethical challenges and implications. This conversation highlights the importance of marketing professionals continually adapting and educating themselves to stay relevant in an ever-changing landscape.

2. "The Future of Digital Advertising": Discussion with Marc Dubois, Pioneer of Programmatic Advertising

Context: Digital advertising is constantly evolving, and programmatic advertising is at the forefront of this transformation. To explore this topic, an in-depth discussion was conducted with Marc Dubois, a recognized expert and pioneer in the field of programmatic advertising.

Discussion Objective: The objective was to understand current and future trends in digital advertising, particularly programmatic advertising, and to gain insights on how businesses can adapt and benefit from these developments.

Key Discussion Points:

1. **Current State of Programmatic Advertising:**

   o   Marc Dubois began by explaining how programmatic advertising has revolutionized the digital advertising landscape, allowing advertisers to buy ad space in a more efficient and targeted way through automation and data analysis.

2. **Challenges and Opportunities:**

   o   He highlighted the challenges facing programmatic advertising, particularly in terms of privacy and data transparency. However, he also highlighted the immense opportunities it offers in terms of precise targeting and performance measurement.

3. **Impact of Artificial Intelligence:**

   o   Dubois discussed the growing impact of AI in programmatic advertising, including for real-time bidding optimization, ad personalization, and predicting consumer behaviors.

4. **Future of Digital Advertising:**

   o   He shared his vision for the future of digital advertising, predicting an increase in the use of augmented and virtual reality, as well as the emergence of new interactive advertising formats.

5. **Tips for Advertisers:**

o   Marc Dubois advised advertisers to stay up to date with the latest technologies and trends, focus on creating quality content and adopt a consumer-centric approach to stay competitive.

6. **Evolution of Marketing Skills:**

o   He   also   discussed the evolving skills required in digital marketing, highlighting the importance of understanding emerging technologies, data analysis and creativity.

Discussion Conclusion: The discussion with Marc Dubois offered valuable perspectives on the rapid evolution of digital advertising and the crucial role of programmatic advertising. Its insights highlight the importance of businesses adapting to technological changes, upholding ethical standards, and focusing on creating advertising campaigns that resonate with their audiences. This conversation highlights that while technology is a key driver, creativity and consumer understanding remain at the heart of digital advertising success.

3. "Winning Content Strategies": Advice from Julia Renard, Editor-

in-Chief and Content Strategist

Background: In a digital world where content is king, developing an effective content strategy is crucial to the success of any online business. Julia Renard, an experienced editor and content strategist, shares her tips on creating winning content strategies.

Interview Objective: The objective was to gather practical tips and proven strategies for creating engaging, informative and influential content that can captivate audiences and promote business growth.

Key Points of the Interview:

1. **Understanding the Audience:**

   o   Julia Renard highlighted the importance of deeply understanding the target audience. She advises conducting in-depth research to capture the interests, needs and preferences of the audience, in order to create content that truly resonates with them.

2. **Creation of Quality Content:**

   o   She emphasized the importance of quality over quantity. Content must be well researched, well written and provide real value. She recommends using stories and real-life examples to make content more relatable and memorable.

3. **Coherence and Branding:**

   o   Julia emphasized the importance of

maintaining consistency in tone, style and messaging to strengthen brand identity. Each piece of content should reflect the brand's personality and values.

4. **Optimization for SEO:**

○ She advised incorporating SEO strategies into content creation to improve online visibility. This includes using relevant keywords, creating catchy titles, and producing content that answers common user questions.

5. **Use of Social Media:**

○ Julia recommended using social media to promote content and engage directly with the audience. She suggests varying formats (posts, videos, infographics) to maintain engagement.

6. **Measurement and Analysis:**

○ She emphasized the importance of regularly measuring content performance using analytics tools. Understanding what works and what doesn't allows you to adjust the strategy accordingly.

Interview Conclusion: The interview with Julia Renard offers valuable insights into creating effective content strategies. His advice highlights the importance of understanding the audience, producing quality content, maintaining brand consistency, optimizing for SEO, using social media for engagement, and measuring performance for continuous adjustments. These strategies are essential for any business looking to establish a strong online presence and authentically connect with their audience.

4. "The Power of Augmented Reality": Perspectives from Alex Tremblay, Innovator in AR and VR

Context: Augmented reality (AR) and virtual reality (VR) are transforming many industries, providing immersive and interactive experiences. Alex Tremblay, a recognized innovator in the field of AR and VR, shares his perspectives on the impact and applications of these technologies.

Interview Objective: The objective was to explore the possibilities offered by AR and VR, particularly in the context of marketing and customer engagement, and to understand how businesses can leverage these technologies to improve their business strategies.

Key Points of the Interview:

1. **Potential of AR and VR:**
   o Alex Tremblay began by highlighting the immense potential of AR and VR to create captivating customer experiences. He explained how these technologies allow users to immerse themselves in virtual environments or enhance their current reality with digital information.

2. Applications in Marketing:

o   Tremblay discussed the applications of AR and VR in marketing, including virtual product trials, immersive store or property tours, and interactive advertising campaigns.

3. Challenges and Solutions:

o   He discussed the technical and financial challenges of adopting AR and VR, while emphasizing the importance of developing engaging and accessible content to ensure successful consumer adoption.

4. Impact on Customer Experience:

o   Tremblay explained how AR and VR can enrich the customer experience, providing opportunities for interaction and engagement that go beyond traditional methods.

5. Future of AR and VR:

o   He shared his vision for the future of these technologies, foreseeing further integration into daily life and continued improvement in their accessibility and ease of use.

6. Advice for Businesses:

o   Alex Tremblay advised companies interested in AR and VR to start with pilot projects to test consumer interest and response, while remaining attentive to technological developments and industry best practices.

Interview Conclusion: The interview with Alex Tremblay offers valuable insights into the transformative potential of AR and VR, particularly in the area of marketing and customer engagement. His insights highlight the importance for businesses to understand these technologies, explore their practical applications, and integrate them strategically to enrich the customer experience and stand out in a competitive market.

5. "Blockchain and Marketing": Vision of the Future with Anil Gupta, Blockchain Expert

Context: Blockchain, often associated with cryptocurrencies, has applications well beyond finance. Anil Gupta, an expert in blockchain technology, explores its potential in the field of marketing.

Interview Objective: The objective was to understand how blockchain can transform marketing, in terms of transparency, data security and new campaign opportunities.

Key Points of the Interview:

1. **Introduction to Blockchain in Marketing:**

   o Anil Gupta started by

explaining the basics of blockchain and how its decentralized and secure nature can benefit marketing. He highlighted the importance of transparency and traceability that blockchain can bring to marketing campaigns.

2. **Practical Applications:**

o Gupta discussed real-world applications of blockchain in marketing, such as securely managing customer data, transparently tracking supply chains for marketing products, and creating more efficient and secure loyalty programs.

3. **Personalization and Privacy:**

o He highlighted how blockchain can balance marketing personalization with data privacy. By using blockchain, businesses can deliver personalized experiences while giving consumers greater control over their data.

4. **Impact on Digital Advertising:**

o Gupta discussed the potential impact of blockchain on digital advertising, including reducing ad fraud and improving campaign transparency.

5. **Challenges and Limitations:**

o He also discussed the challenges of adopting blockchain in marketing, such as technological complexity, the need for standardization, and regulatory issues.

6. **Vision of the Future:**

○ In conclusion, Anil Gupta shared his vision for the future of blockchain in marketing. He foresees increasing adoption of blockchain, leading to more transparent, secure and consumer-centric campaigns.

Interview Conclusion: The interview with Anil Gupta offers an in-depth perspective on the revolutionary potential of blockchain in marketing. Its insights reveal how this technology can transform the way businesses manage customer data, run advertising campaigns and build trust with their audiences. For marketers, understanding and adopting blockchain could be a key factor in remaining competitive in an ever-changing digital future.

6. "E-Commerce Revolution": Insights from Mia Zhang, CEO of E-Shop Innovations

Context: E-commerce has undergone rapid and continuous transformation, profoundly influencing consumer purchasing habits. Mia Zhang, CEO of E-Shop Innovations, a leading e-commerce solutions company, shares her insights on current and future industry trends.

Interview Objective: The objective was to gather expert perspectives on the e-commerce revolution, focusing on technological innovations, digital marketing strategies, and evolving consumer expectations.

Key Points of the Interview:

1. Evolution of Electronic Commerce:

o　　　Mia Zhang began by discussing the rapid evolution of e-commerce, highlighting how technology has changed the way people buy and sell products. It highlighted the growing importance of user experience in e-commerce platforms.

2. Technological innovations :

o　　　Zhang spoke about the latest innovations, such as artificial intelligence, augmented reality, and chatbots, which are transforming the online shopping experience by making it more interactive and personalized.

3. Digital Marketing Strategies:

o　　She shared insights on effective digital marketing strategies in e-commerce, including the importance of SEO, content marketing, and social media to attract and retain customers.

4. Consumer Behavior:

o　　Zhang discussed changing consumer behaviors, emphasizing the growing demand for fast, secure and personalized online shopping experiences.

5. Challenges and Opportunities:

- She addressed the challenges facing online retailers, including managing logistics, increased competition, and the need for constant adaptation to new technologies.

6. **Future of Electronic Commerce:**

- In conclusion, Mia Zhang shared her vision for the future of e-commerce, foreseeing further integration of advanced technologies and an increased focus on personalized and omnichannel customer experience.

Interview Conclusion: The interview with Mia Zhang offers valuable insights into the ever-changing dynamics of e-commerce. Its insights highlight the importance of technological innovation and deep understanding of consumer behavior to succeed in modern e-commerce. For companies operating in this sector, staying at the forefront of technology and quickly adapting to market changes are essential to remaining competitive and effectively meeting consumer needs.

7. "Social Media Engagement": Strategies from Laura Martinez, Social Media Consultant

Context: In a world where social media has become a central part of communication and marketing, engagement on these platforms is crucial for business success. Laura Martinez, an experienced social media consultant, shares her strategies for maximizing engagement and building brands' online presence.

Interview Objective: The objective was to gather effective strategies and practical tips for improving social media engagement, focusing on best practices for connecting with audiences and building brand visibility.

Key Points of the Interview:

1. **Understanding the Audience:**
   - Laura Martinez emphasized the importance of deeply understanding the target audience. She recommends analyzing demographics, interests, and behaviors to create content that resonates with the audience.

2. **Quality and Consistent Content:**
   - She insisted on the need to produce quality content, consistent and aligned with the brand identity. Content should be informative, entertaining and engaging to encourage interaction.

3. **Interaction and Responsiveness:**
   - Martinez advised responding quickly to comments and messages to build trust with the audience. Regular interaction increases subscriber engagement and loyalty.

4. Use of Platform Features:

o   She recommended making full use of the features offered by each platform, such as Instagram Stories, Twitter Polls, or Facebook Live Video, to diversify content and increase engagement.

5. Campaigns and Collaborations:

o   Laura suggested running interactive campaigns, like contests or challenges, and collaborating with influencers to expand reach and attract new followers.

6. Measurement and Analysis:

o   She highlighted the importance of regularly measuring performance using analytics tools to understand what is working and what is not, allowing the strategy to be adjusted accordingly.

Interview Conclusion: The interview with Laura Martinez offers valuable insights on optimizing social media engagement. His advice highlights the importance of understanding the audience, creating quality content, actively interacting with subscribers, leveraging platform features, and measuring the impact of actions taken. For brands looking to strengthen their online presence, adopting these strategies can lead to a significant increase in engagement and improved visibility on social media.

8. "Data Analysis for Marketing":

Advanced Techniques with Dr. Rajesh Kumar, Data Scientist

Background: Data analytics plays a crucial role in modern marketing, enabling businesses to make informed decisions and optimize their strategies. Dr. Rajesh Kumar, a renowned data scientist, shares his insights on using advanced data analytics techniques in marketing.

Interview Objective: The objective was to explore the methods and applications of advanced data analytics in marketing, focusing on how businesses can use these techniques to improve the effectiveness of their campaigns marketing.

Key Points of the Interview:

1. **Importance of Data Analysis:**
   o   Dr. Kumar began by highlighting the importance of data analytics in understanding consumer behavior and measuring the effectiveness of marketing campaigns.

2. **Advanced Analysis Techniques:**
   o   He discussed advanced techniques such as machine learning, predictive analytics, and natural language processing. These techniques make it possible to identify trends, predict consumer behavior and optimize campaigns in real time.

3. **Marketing Personalization:**
   o   Dr. Kumar explained how data analytics enables further personalization

of marketing campaigns, targeting consumers with messages and offers tailored to their individual needs and preferences.

4. **Market segmentation :**

o   He highlighted the importance of data-driven market segmentation, allowing businesses to target specific groups more effectively.

5. **Performance Measurement:**

o   Dr. Kumar discussed methods for measuring and analyzing the performance of marketing campaigns, using key performance indicators (KPIs) to assess return on investment (ROI).

6. **Challenges and Solutions:**

o   He also discussed the challenges of data analytics, such as managing large amounts of data and ensuring consumer privacy is protected.

Interview Conclusion: The interview with Dr. Rajesh Kumar offers valuable insights on the application of advanced data analytics in marketing. Its insights highlight the importance of strategically using data to understand consumers, personalize campaigns, and measure the effectiveness of marketing efforts. For businesses looking to optimize their marketing strategies, adopting these advanced data analysis techniques is essential to remaining competitive in an increasingly data-driven business environment.

9. "Personalization in the Digital Age": Interview with Emily Robinson, Personalized Marketing Expert

Background: Personalization has become a key part of digital marketing, allowing businesses to connect with their customers in a more meaningful and effective way. Emily Robinson, a personalized marketing expert, shares her insights on best practices and trends in this area.

Interview Objective: The objective was to understand how businesses can use personalization to improve customer engagement, increase conversions and build brand loyalty in today's digital environment.

Key Points of the Interview:

1. **Importance of Personalization:**
   - Emily Robinson began by highlighting the growing importance of personalization in digital marketing. She explained how personalization can improve the customer experience by making interactions more relevant and engaging.

2. **Use of Data for Personalization:**
   - She discussed using customer data

to create personalized experiences. This includes analyzing purchasing behaviors, preferences and past interactions to offer tailored recommendations and content.

3. **Personalization Technologies:**

o   Robinson discussed the different technologies that facilitate personalization, such as artificial intelligence, machine learning, and marketing automation, which enable personalization at scale.

4. **Personalized Content Strategies:**

o   She shared strategies for creating effective personalized content, emphasizing the importance of understanding the unique needs and desires of each customer segment.

5. **Customization Challenges:**

o   Emily also discussed the challenges of personalization, including managing data privacy and balancing personalization with information overload.

6. **Future of Personalization:**

o   In conclusion, she shared her vision for the future of personalization in digital marketing, predicting an increase in the adoption of advanced technologies and even more refined and integrated personalization.

Interview Conclusion: The interview with

Emily Robinson offers valuable insights into personalization in digital marketing. His advice highlights the importance of strategically using data and technology to create personalized and memorable customer experiences. For businesses looking to stand out in a crowded digital landscape, adopting advanced personalization strategies is essential to effectively engage customers and build brand loyalty.

10. "SEO and Online Visibility": Tips from Kevin Patel, SEO Guru

Context: In a digital world where online visibility is essential for business success, natural referencing (SEO) plays a crucial role. Kevin Patel, a recognized SEO expert, shares his tips and strategies for improving businesses' online visibility.

Interview Objective: The aim was to gather practical tips and proven strategies for optimizing SEO and improving businesses' online presence, focusing on best practices for increasing organic traffic and search engine visibility. of research.

Key Points of the Interview:

1. **Importance of SEO:**
   - Kevin Patel started by highlighting the importance of SEO in today's digital marketing. He explained how good SEO can lead to increased visibility, quality traffic and better online credibility.

2. **Keyword Search:**
o   Patel emphasized the importance of keyword research to understand what the target audience is looking for. He advised using keyword research tools to identify relevant, high-potential terms.

3. **On-Page Optimization:**
o   He shared tips for on-page optimization, including creating compelling titles and meta descriptions, using H1 and H2 tags properly, and optimizing images.

4. **Quality Content:**
o   Kevin stressed the importance of producing quality content that is informative and relevant to the audience. He recommended creating content that answers user questions and adds value.

5. **Technical SEO:**
o   He touched on the technical side of SEO, talking about the importance of site loading speed, mobile compatibility and clean URL structure.

6. **Backlinks and Domain Authority:**
o   Patel discussed the importance of backlinks for building domain authority. He advised adopting ethical link building strategies to get quality links from authoritative sites.

7. **Measurement and Analysis:**
o   Finally, he highlighted the

importance of measuring and analyzing SEO performance using tools like Google Analytics and Google Search Console to understand what is working and what can be improved.

Interview Conclusion: The interview with Kevin Patel offers valuable insights on optimizing SEO to improve online visibility. His advice highlights the importance of a well-planned SEO strategy, including keyword research, on-page optimization, quality content creation, technical aspects, and a solid backlink strategy. For businesses looking to increase their online presence, following these tips can lead to a significant improvement in their search engine visibility and an increase in their organic traffic.

11. "Mobile Marketing and Applications": Trends and Advice from Omar Farooq, Mobile Application Developer

Background: With the steady increase in smartphone usage, mobile marketing and apps have become essential tools for reaching consumers. Omar Farooq, an experienced mobile app developer, shares his perspectives on the latest trends and offers tips for success in mobile marketing.

Interview Objective: The objective was to explore

current and future mobile marketing strategies, focusing on how businesses can use mobile apps to improve customer engagement and drive sales.

Key Points of the Interview:

1. **Growing Importance of Mobile Marketing:**
   - Omar Farooq began by highlighting the growing importance of mobile marketing in today's landscape. He explained how smartphones have become a preferred communication channel for many consumers.

2. **Mobile Application Development:**
   - Farooq shared insights on mobile app development, emphasizing the importance of creating intuitive, fast and engaging apps that deliver real value to users.

3. **Personalization and User Experience:**
   - He highlighted the importance of personalization in mobile applications to improve user experience. Farooq advised using user data to deliver personalized and relevant experiences.

4. **Integration of Advanced Features:**
   - Omar discussed integrating advanced features such as augmented reality, chatbots and artificial intelligence to enrich user experience and increase engagement.

5. **Monetization Strategies:**

o　　He discussed different monetization strategies for mobile apps, including in-app purchases, subscriptions, and targeted advertising.

6. **Importance of Updates and Support:**

o　　Farooq emphasized the importance of keeping apps updated with the latest features and providing timely support to improve user satisfaction.

7. **Future Trends in Mobile Marketing:**

o　　　In conclusion, he shared his vision for future trends in mobile marketing, foreseeing an increase in the use of emerging technologies to create more immersive and interactive user experiences.

Interview Conclusion: The interview with Omar Farooq offers valuable perspectives on mobile marketing and app development. His advice highlights the importance of creating user-centric mobile apps that integrate advanced features and deliver personalized experiences. For businesses looking to stand out in a crowded mobile market, adopting these strategies can lead to significantly improved customer engagement and increased revenue.

12. "Influencers and Brands": Effective Collaboration with Sarah Johnson,

Influencer Marketing Specialist

Context: Influencer marketing has become a key part of brand strategies in today's digital world. Sarah Johnson, a renowned expert in influencer marketing, shares her insights on how brands can effectively collaborate with influencers to maximize their impact.

Interview Objective: The objective was to explore best practices for collaborations between brands and influencers, focusing on creating partnerships that are authentic and beneficial to both parties.

Key Points of the Interview:

1. **Choice of Influencers:**
   - Sarah Johnson began by emphasizing the importance of choosing influencers whose image and values match those of the brand. She advised analyzing the influencer's audience, engagement and credibility before establishing a partnership.

2. **Developing Authentic Relationships:**
   - She emphasized the importance of developing authentic relationships with influencers. This involves working with influencers who are truly passionate about the brand and its products.

3. **Content Strategies:**
   - Johnson discussed content strategies for influencer campaigns, recommending allowing influencers to have some creative

freedom to produce content that naturally resonates with their audience.

4. **Impact Measurement:**

o　　　　　　　　She discussed the importance of measuring the impact of influencer campaigns, using metrics such as engagement, reach, and return on investment (ROI).

5. **Trends and Innovations:**

o　　　　　Sarah shared her insight into current and future trends in influencer marketing, including the growing use of micro-influencers and the integration of augmented and virtual reality into campaigns.

6. **Challenges and Solutions:**

o　　She also discussed common challenges in brand and influencer collaborations, such as managing expectations and maintaining authenticity, and offered solutions to overcome them.

Interview Conclusion: The interview with Sarah Johnson offers valuable insights into brand and influencer collaborations in today's marketing. His advice highlights the importance of choosing the right influencers, developing authentic relationships, creating engaging content, and measuring the impact of campaigns. For brands looking to leverage influencer marketing, following these strategies can lead to more successful partnerships and greater resonance with their target audience.

13. "User Experience and Web Design": Key Principles with Diego Martinez, UX/UI Designer

Background: User experience (UX) and user interface (UI) are crucial to the success of any digital product. Diego Martinez, an experienced UX/UI designer, shares his key principles for creating engaging and intuitive web experiences.

Interview Objective: The objective was to explore best practices in UX/UI design, focusing on how to create websites and applications that meet user needs while being aesthetically pleasing.

Key Points of the Interview:

1. **User Understanding:**
   o   Diego Martinez began by emphasizing the importance of understanding user needs, wants and behaviors. He recommended extensive user research, including interviews and usability testing, to guide the design.

2. **Simplicity and Clarity:**
   o   He emphasized the need to maintain simplicity and clarity in the design. This includes using intuitive navigation, reducing cognitive overload, and creating clean interfaces.

3. Consistency in Design:

o   Martinez spoke about the importance of consistency in design, using recurring design elements, harmonious color palettes, and uniform typography to create a consistent user experience.

4. Responsive Design:

o   He discussed the importance of responsive design, ensuring websites and apps work well on a variety of devices and screen sizes.

5. Accessibility:

o   Diego highlighted the importance of accessibility in UX/UI design, ensuring that digital products are usable by people with diverse abilities.

6. Testing and Iteration:

o   He recommended continuous testing with real users and iteration based on feedback to constantly improve the user experience.

7. Trends and Innovations:

o   In conclusion, Martinez shared his perspective on current and future trends in UX/UI, such as the adoption of artificial intelligence, designing for wearables, and augmented reality.

Interview Conclusion: The interview with Diego Martinez offers valuable insights into UX/UI design. Its key principles highlight the importance of understanding users, creating simple and consistent designs, ensuring accessibility, and adopting an iterative approach based on testing. For designers and developers looking to create exceptional web and mobile experiences, following these guidelines can lead to more intuitive, engaging, and successful products.

14. "Sustainable Development and Marketing": Ethical Approaches with Nora Khaled, Sustainable Development Consultant

Context: In a world increasingly aware of environmental and social issues, sustainable development has become a crucial aspect of marketing. Nora Khaled, a sustainability consultant, shares her perspectives on integrating sustainable and ethical practices into marketing strategies.

Objective of the Interview: The objective was to explore how companies can adopt marketing approaches that not only respect the principles of sustainable development, but also contribute to a positive and responsible brand image.

Key Points of the Interview:

1. **Importance of Sustainable Development in Marketing:**

   o   Nora Khaled highlighted the growing importance of sustainability in consumer decisions. She explained how a sustainable approach can strengthen a brand's reputation and foster customer loyalty.

2. **Transparency and Authenticity:**

o　　　She emphasized the need for brands to be transparent and authentic in their sustainable practices. This includes honest communication about sustainability efforts and environmental impacts.

3. **Green Marketing and Communication:**

o　　Khaled discussed green marketing strategies, recommending highlighting the company's green initiatives in marketing communications, while avoiding greenwashing.

4. **Commitment to Social Responsibility:**

o　　She highlighted the importance of corporate social engagement, encouraging brands to support relevant social and environmental causes.

5. **Sustainable Innovation:**

o　　　Nora addressed the importance of innovation in developing sustainable products and services, encouraging businesses to integrate sustainable practices from the design phase.

6. **Partnerships and Collaborations:**

o　　　She advised forming partnerships

with sustainable organizations and environmental groups to strengthen the credibility and impact of sustainability initiatives.

7. **Impact Measurement:**

○   Khaled highlighted the importance of measuring and communicating the impact of sustainable initiatives, using clear metrics to demonstrate the company's commitment to sustainability.

Interview Conclusion: The interview with Nora Khaled offers valuable insights on integrating sustainability into marketing. His advice highlights the importance of transparency, authenticity, sustainable innovation, and social engagement for brands wishing to adopt ethical marketing practices. For businesses looking to position themselves as responsible and environmentally conscious, following these strategies can not only improve their brand image, but also contribute positively to society and the environment.

Models and Examples of Strategies

Strategic Planning Models

Strategic planning is essential for any business wishing to successfully navigate the ever-changing business landscape. Here is a guide to strategic planning models that can be used to structure and guide the process of developing effective strategies.

1. **SWOT Analysis (Strengths, Weaknesses, Opportunities, Threats):**
   o This model involves evaluating your company's internal strengths and weaknesses, as well as external opportunities and threats. It helps identify key areas to focus on to improve and grow your business.

2. **SMART objectives (Specific, Measurable, Achievable, Realistic, Timely defined):**
   o SMART goals help set clear, achievable targets for your business. This model ensures that each goal is specific, measurable, achievable, realistic and time-bound.

3. **Porter's Five Forces Model:**
   o This model analyzes five forces that influence competitiveness in an industry: the threat of new entrants, the bargaining power of suppliers, the bargaining power of customers, the threat of substitute products or services, and the intensity of competitive competition .

4. **Scenario-Based Planning:**
   o Scenario-based planning involves creating different possible future

scenarios. This helps businesses consider various possibilities and develop flexible strategies that can adapt to unforeseen changes.

5. **McKinsey 7S model:**

o   This model examines seven interrelated elements that make up an organization: structure, strategy, systems, style, people, skills and shared values. It is used to ensure that all aspects of the business are aligned and working together effectively.

6. **Ansoff Strategic Planning Model:**

o   The Ansoff model, or growth matrix, helps companies determine their growth strategy by evaluating market and product options, including market penetration, market development, product development and diversification.

7. **Boston Consulting Group (BCG) Strategic Planning Model:**

o   The BCG Matrix is a strategic planning tool that helps companies evaluate their product or business unit portfolios based on their market share and market growth rate.

8. **Balanced Scorecard Strategic Planning Model:**

o   The Balanced Scorecard is a strategic management framework used to track and manage organizational performance by focusing on key indicators from four perspectives: financial, customer, internal processes, and learning and growth.

9. **Blue Ocean Strategic Planning Model:**

o   The Blue Ocean model encourages companies to move out of saturated markets (red oceans) and create new market spaces (blue oceans) where competition is less intense.

10. **PESTEL Strategic Planning Model:**

o   PESTEL analysis examines the Political, Economic, Social, Technological, Environmental and Legal factors that can affect a business. It is used to identify external trends that can influence company strategy.

Each of these models offers a unique approach to helping businesses develop effective strategies and plan for the future. By using them, businesses can better understand their environment, identify growth opportunities and prepare for future challenges.

Examples of Digital Marketing Strategies

Digital marketing is a dynamic and constantly evolving field. Here are real-world examples of digital marketing strategies that can be applied to improve visibility, engagement and conversion.

1. **Search Engine Optimization (SEO):**

o **Example:** A fashion company implements a comprehensive SEO strategy, including keyword research to identify the most searched terms in its sector, optimization of its website content, and building quality links to improve its ranking in search results.

2. **Content Marketing:**

o **Example:** A sports equipment manufacturer develops a content-rich blog, offering training tips, product reviews and inspiring stories from athletes. Content is regularly shared on social media to increase engagement and drive traffic to the site.

3. **Social Media Marketing:**

o **Example:** A tech startup uses social media to share product updates, customer testimonials, and demo videos. She also engages her audience through live Q&As and competitions.

4. **Paid Advertising (PPC):**

o **Example:** A local restaurant launches a paid advertising campaign on Google Ads and Facebook, targeting specific keywords and local audiences to promote its specials and increase bookings.

5. **Email Marketing:**

o **Example:** An online bookstore creates a monthly newsletter offering book reviews, author interviews, and exclusive discounts. It segments its subscriber list to personalize reading recommendations based on each subscriber's interests.

6. **Influencer Marketing:**
○ **Example:** A cosmetics brand collaborates with influencers on Instagram and YouTube to create content around its products. Influencers share their experience with the products and offer discount codes to their followers.

7. **Video Content Strategies:**
○ **Example:** A fitness company creates a series of workout and wellness tips videos on YouTube, attracting an engaged audience and increasing brand awareness.

8. **Mobile Optimization and Application Marketing:**
○ **Example:** A food delivery app optimizes its website and app for mobile devices, providing a seamless user experience. It also uses targeted advertising campaigns to encourage downloads of the app.

9. **Automated Marketing Strategies:**
○ **Example:** A B2B service provider uses automation tools to track leads, send personalized emails based on user behavior, and nurture prospects throughout the customer journey.

10. **Use of Data and Analytics for Decision**

Making:

- **Example:** An online retailer uses analytics tools to track user behavior on its site, identify the most popular products, and adjust its inventory and marketing strategy accordingly.

These examples illustrate how different digital marketing strategies can be applied in various contexts to achieve specific goals, improve customer engagement, and drive business growth.

Influencer Marketing Strategies

Influencer marketing is a key strategy in today's digital world, allowing brands to connect with their target audience through influential figures on social media. Here are detailed strategies for implementing effective influencer marketing.

1. **Identification and Selection of Relevant Influencers:**

- **Strategy:** Look for influencers whose target audience matches that of your brand. Use social media analytics tools to assess their reach, engagement, and relevance. Favor influencers whose style and values match those of your brand.

2. **Developing Authentic Relationships with Influencers:**

- **Strategy:** Build long-term relationships with influencers. Start with authentic interactions on their platforms, like commenting on their posts or sharing their content, before offering them a partnership.

3. **Creation of Collaborative Content:**

o **Strategy:** Work with influencers to create content that feels natural and authentic to their usual style. The content should provide value to their audience while highlighting your brand in a subtle way.

4. **Targeted Campaigns Based on Events or Launches:**

o **Strategy:** Use influencer marketing for specific campaigns, like a new product launch or special event. Influencers can create buzz around the event and draw attention to your brand.

5. **Use of Promo Codes and Tracking Links:**

o **Strategy:** Provide influencers with exclusive promo codes or tracking links. This not only helps measure the effectiveness of the campaign, but also provides a tangible incentive for their audience to engage with your brand.

6. **Multiplatform Engagement:**

o **Strategy:** Involve influencers across multiple platforms (Instagram, YouTube, TikTok, etc.) to maximize reach. Adapt content to each platform for better resonance with the target audience.

7. **Performance Analysis and**

Measurement:

o **Strategy:** Use analytics tools to track the performance of influencer marketing campaigns. Measure engagement, reach, traffic generated and conversions to assess ROI and adjust future strategies.

8. **Influencer Marketing and CSR (Corporate Social Responsibility):**

o **Strategy:** Integrate CSR initiatives into your influencer marketing campaigns. Collaborate with influencers on projects that highlight your brand's sustainability or social responsibility efforts.

9. **Narratives and Storytelling:**

o **Strategy:** Encourage influencers to tell compelling stories around your brand. Storytelling can create a deeper emotional connection with the audience.

10. **Innovation and Trends:**

o **Strategy:** Stay on top of the latest influencer marketing trends, like using virtual influencers or leveraging new social media features, to keep your campaigns fresh and engaging.

By implementing these strategies, businesses can take full advantage of influencer marketing to increase awareness, engage their target audience, and boost conversions.

SEO Strategy Templates

Search Engine Optimization (SEO) is a crucial part of digital marketing, helping websites improve their visibility and search engine rankings. Here are some SEO strategy templates you can adopt to optimize your online presence.

1. **On-Page Optimization:**

o **Strategy:** Focus on optimizing individual elements of your website, such as titles, meta descriptions, quality content, and strategic use of keywords. Make sure each page is optimized for specific, relevant keywords.

2. **Technical Optimization:**

o **Strategy:** Improve the technical aspects of your website to make it more accessible to search engines. This includes improving site speed, creating an XML sitemap file, optimizing URLs, and ensuring your site is mobile-friendly.

3. **Creation of Quality Content:**

o **Strategy:** Develop informative, relevant, high-quality content that addresses the needs and questions of your target audience. Use a variety of formats like blog posts, videos, infographics and case studies.

4. **Link Building:**

o **Strategy:** Focus on acquiring quality backlinks from authoritative websites. Use techniques like guest blogging, partnering with other sites, and creating shareable content that naturally attracts links.

5. **Local SEO:**
o   **Strategy:** If you have a brick-and-mortar business or local audience, optimize your online presence for local searches. This includes creating a Google My Business page, optimizing for local keywords, and collecting customer reviews.

6. **Competition analysis :**
o   **Strategy:** Analyze your competitors' SEO strategies to identify opportunities and gaps in your own strategy. Use tools to analyze the keywords they rank for, the backlinks they have acquired, and their content performance.

7. **Optimization for Voice Search:**
o   **Strategy:** Optimize your content for voice search by using natural language and key phrases in the form of questions. Focus on long-tail queries and direct answers to common questions.

8. **Performance Monitoring and Analysis:**
o   **Strategy:** Use tools like Google Analytics and Google Search Console to track your site's performance. Analyze metrics such as organic traffic, bounce rate, and ranking positions to adjust your SEO strategy.

9. **Mobile SEO:**

o **Strategy:** Make sure your site is fully optimized for mobile devices. This includes responsive design, fast loading times, and a smooth mobile user experience.

10. **Use of Structured Data:**

o **Strategy:** Implement structured data (schema markup) to help search engines better understand the content of your site. This can improve how your pages are displayed in search results with rich snippets.

By implementing these SEO strategies, you can significantly improve the visibility of your website in search engines, attract more qualified traffic, and ultimately increase your conversion rate.

Sustainable Development Strategies

Sustainability has become a crucial aspect of business strategy, not only for its positive contribution to the environment and society, but also for its ability to generate long-term value for the company. Here are sustainability strategies businesses can adopt to integrate responsible practices into their operations.

1. **Environmental Impact Assessment:**

o **Strategy:** Conduct a comprehensive environmental impact assessment of your business. This includes the analysis of energy consumption, greenhouse gas emissions, water use, and waste management. Use this data to identify areas for improvement.

2. **Reduction of the Carbon Footprint:**

o **Strategy:** Implement measures to reduce your company's carbon footprint. This can include using renewable energy, improving the energy efficiency of buildings and processes, and reducing travel by promoting teleworking or sustainable business travel.

3. **Sustainable Resource Management:**

o **Strategy:** Adopt sustainable resource management practices. This may involve reducing the consumption of raw materials, recycling materials, and using recycled or biodegradable products.

4. **Responsible Supply Chain:**

o **Strategy:** Make sure your supply chain is ethical and sustainable. This includes choosing suppliers who adhere to environmental and social standards, and implementing responsible sourcing policies.

5. **Commitment to CSR (Corporate Social Responsibility):**

o **Strategy:** Develop and implement CSR initiatives that align with your company values. This may include employee volunteer programs, donations to social causes, and partnerships with nonprofit organizations.

6. **Sustainable Innovation:**

o   **Strategy:** Encourage sustainable innovation within your company. Invest in research and development of eco-friendly products and services, and explore new, more sustainable production methods.

7. **Communication and Transparency:**

o   **Strategy:** Openly communicate your sustainability commitments and achievements. Publish sustainability reports and use your communications platforms to raise awareness of your efforts.

8. **Training and Awareness of Employees:**

o   **Strategy:** Train and raise awareness among your employees about sustainable development practices. Encourage them to adopt eco-responsible behaviors at work and in their personal lives.

9. **Integration of Sustainable Development into Corporate Culture:**

o   **Strategy:** Make sustainability an integral part of your company culture. This may include establishing sustainable internal policies and encouraging a sustainability mindset at all levels of the organization.

10. **Collaboration and Partnerships:**

o   **Strategy:** Collaborate with other businesses, governments, and non-governmental organizations to promote sustainable development initiatives. Partnerships can help share knowledge, resources and achieve greater impact.

By adopting these sustainability strategies, businesses can not only contribute positively to the environment and society, but also strengthen their brand, improve their competitiveness and ensure their long-term viability.

Customer Personalization Strategies

Customer personalization is a key strategy for improving customer experience, increasing loyalty and driving sales. Here are customer personalization strategies businesses can adopt to deliver more targeted and relevant experiences.

1. **Collection and Analysis of Customer Data:**

o   **Strategy:** Use data analytics tools to collect information about customer preferences, purchasing behavior, and past interactions. Analyze this data to understand the specific needs and interests of your customers.

2. **Audience Segmentation:**

o   **Strategy:** Divide your customer base into segments based on criteria such as age, gender, geographic location, purchasing behavior, and interests. This allows you to create more targeted and relevant marketing messages.

3. **Content Personalization:**

o   **Strategy:** Create personalized content that resonates with different customer segments. This can include personalized emails, product recommendations on your website, and social media posts tailored to user interests.

4. **Personalized User Experience on the Website:**

o   **Strategy:** Use technology to tailor the experience on your website based on visitor preferences and behavior. This may include displaying specific products or offers, and personalizing site navigation.

5. **Targeted Email Marketing:**

o   **Strategy:** Send personalized emails based on customer actions and preferences. Use marketing automation tools to send relevant messages at the right time, like abandoned cart emails or birthday specials.

6. **Personalized Offers and Promotions:**

o   **Strategy:** Create offers and promotions that are personalized for specific customer segments. This could include discounts on products they've viewed or offers based on their previous purchases.

7. **Chatbots and Personalized Assistance:**

o   **Strategy:** Use chatbots and virtual assistants to offer personalized assistance. Chatbots can answer customer questions, recommend products, and provide tailored support.

8. **Feedback and Listening to Customers:**

o   **Strategy:** Collect regular feedback from your customers and use this information to improve personalization. Surveys, social media comments, and customer reviews are valuable sources of information.

9. **Use of Artificial Intelligence:**

o   **Strategy:** Implement AI solutions to analyze customer data at scale and generate insights for personalization. AI can help identify trends and patterns in customer behavior.

10. **Consistent Omnichannel Experiences:**

o   **Strategy:** Ensure a consistent experience across all channels – online and offline. Personalization should be integrated into the website, mobile applications, in-store interactions, and marketing campaigns.

By adopting these customer personalization strategies, businesses can create more engaging and relevant experiences for their customers, which can lead to increased customer satisfaction, loyalty and sales.

Programmatic Advertising Strategies

Programmatic advertising uses automated platforms to buy and sell advertising space online, allowing advertisers to target their audiences more precisely and efficiently. Here are key strategies for optimizing your programmatic advertising campaigns.

1. **Understanding of Programmatic Platforms:**

   o **Strategy:** Familiarize yourself with different programmatic platforms, including DSPs (Demand-Side Platforms), SSPs (Supply-Side Platforms), and ad exchanges. Understanding how these platforms work is essential to optimizing your campaigns.

2. **Precise Audience Targeting:**

   o **Strategy:** Use demographic, behavioral, and contextual data to precisely target your audience. Targeting may include age, gender, interests, browsing behavior, and geographic location.

3. **Real-Time Optimization:**

   o **Strategy:** Take advantage of programmatic advertising's ability to optimize campaigns in real time. Use data analytics to adjust your bidding, targeting, and ad creative based on performance.

4. **Use of the Data Management Platform**

(DMP):

o **Strategy:** Integrate a DMP to centralize and manage your audience data. This will allow you to create more precise audience segments and improve the targeting of your campaigns.

5. **Dynamic Creativity:**

o **Strategy:** Use dynamic ads to personalize ad content based on the user. This can include modifying images, messages, and calls to action based on user data.

6. **Multiplatform Integration:**

o **Strategy:** Make sure your programmatic campaigns are integrated across multiple platforms and devices. This includes desktop, mobile, tablet, and even connected TV platforms.

7. **Respect for Confidentiality and Compliance:**

o **Strategy:** Be aware of data privacy laws and regulations, like GDPR. Make sure your data collection and use practices are compliant.

8. **Analysis and Reporting:**

o **Strategy:** Use analytics tools to track your campaign performance. Analyze metrics such as CTR (Click-Through Rate), conversion rate, and ROI to evaluate the effectiveness of your campaigns.

9. **A/B Testing and Experimentation:**

- o **Strategy:** Conduct A/B testing on different elements of your campaigns, like visuals, ad copy, and calls to action, to determine what resonates best with your audience.

10. **Strategic Partnerships:**
- o **Strategy:** Establish strategic partnerships with publishers or ad networks to access quality ad inventory and specific audiences.

By implementing these strategies, advertisers can maximize the effectiveness of their programmatic advertising campaigns, reach their target audiences more precisely, and improve the ROI of their advertising efforts.

Examples of Mobile Marketing Strategies and Applications

Mobile marketing and apps are powerful tools for reaching and engaging customers in an increasingly connected world. Here are real-world examples of mobile and app marketing strategies that businesses can use to improve engagement and drive sales.

1. **Optimization for Mobile Devices:**
- o **Example:** An online clothing store optimizes its website for mobile devices, ensuring smooth navigation, fast loading times, and an easy shopping experience on smartphones and tablets.

2. **Dedicated Mobile Application:**

o   **Example:** A supermarket is developing a mobile app that allows customers to shop online, receive notifications about special offers, and scan products in-store for additional information.

3. **Marketing by SMS and MMS:**

o   **Example:** A hair salon sends appointment reminders via SMS and promotional offers via MMS to its customers, increasing retention and response rates.

4. **Targeted Mobile Advertising:**

o   **Example:** A restaurant uses targeted mobile ads on platforms like Google and Facebook to reach local customers with special offers and daily menus.

5. **Augmented Reality (AR) Campaigns:**

o   **Example:** A cosmetics brand creates an AR campaign in its app, allowing users to virtually try on different makeup products before purchasing.

6. **In-App Loyalty Programs:**

o   **Example:** A coffee chain offers a loyalty program in its app, where customers can earn points and get rewards for every purchase made through the app.

7. **Personalized Push Notifications:**

o   **Example:** A fitness app sends personalized push notifications to encourage users to achieve their daily health and fitness goals.

8. **Social Media Integration:**

o **Example:** A travel app incorporates social media sharing features, allowing users to easily share their travel experiences and itineraries with their friends.

9. **Use of Artificial Intelligence (AI):**

o **Example:** A customer service application uses AI to offer an interactive chatbot that answers customer questions and provides real-time assistance.

10. **Mobile Influencer Marketing Strategies:**

o **Example:** A fashion brand partners with influencers on Instagram to promote its mobile app, using sponsored posts and stories to attract users to the app.

By implementing these strategies, businesses can take full advantage of the opportunities offered by mobile and app marketing to reach their target audience, improve customer engagement and drive sales.

Customer Relationship Management (CRM) Strategies

Customer relationship management (CRM) is essential for developing and maintaining strong relationships with customers. Here are effective

CRM strategies that businesses can adopt to improve customer engagement, retention, and sales growth.

1. Centralization of Customer Data:

o **Strategy:** Use a CRM system to centralize all customer information, including past interactions, preferences, purchasing data and feedback. This allows a complete view of the customer for personalized service.

2. Customer Segmentation:

o **Strategy:** Segment your customer base in CRM based on various criteria such as purchasing behavior, preferences, location and income level. Segmentation helps target communications and offers more effectively.

3. Automation of Sales and Marketing Processes:

o **Strategy:** Automate repetitive processes like follow-up emails, renewal notifications, and marketing campaigns. Automation saves time and ensures consistent communication.

4. Personalization of Communication:

o **Strategy:** Use CRM data to personalize your interactions with customers. Personalized emails, product recommendations, and special offers can increase customer engagement and satisfaction.

5. **Monitoring and Analysis of Customer Interactions:**

o   **Strategy:** Track and analyze all customer interactions through the CRM to understand their needs and behaviors. Use these insights to improve products, services and customer experiences.

6. **Customer Feedback Management:**

o   **Strategy:** Use CRM to collect and manage customer feedback. Actively respond to comments and use feedback to improve products and services.

7. **Integration of Communication Channels:**

o   **Strategy:** Integrate various communication channels such as email, social media, phone calls and live chat into your CRM. This ensures a consistent and integrated customer experience.

8. **Training and Awareness of Employees:**

o   **Strategy:** Train your employees in the effective use of CRM. Make sure they understand the importance of accurately capturing data and using insights to improve customer interaction.

9. **Development of Loyalty Programs:**

o   **Strategy:** Use CRM to develop and manage loyalty programs. Offer rewards and benefits based on customer purchase history and engagement to encourage loyalty.

10. **Sales Forecasting and Analysis:**

○   **Strategy:** Use CRM data and analytics tools to predict sales trends and adjust strategies accordingly. This can help identify sales opportunities and optimize marketing efforts.

By adopting these CRM strategies, businesses can not only improve their relationship with customers but also increase the efficiency of their sales and marketing teams, leading to sustained business growth.

Examples of Content Strategies

An effective content strategy is essential for engaging audiences, building brand awareness, and improving SEO. Here are real-world examples of content strategies that businesses can use to achieve their marketing goals.

1. **Blogs and Feature Articles:**

○   **Example:** A technology company creates a regularly updated blog with in-depth articles on the latest technology trends, tutorials and case studies. This establishes the brand as an authority in its field and improves its SEO.

2. **Educational and Demonstrative Videos:**

○   **Example:** A cooking brand produces recipe videos and product demonstrations, shared on YouTube and embedded on its website. These videos help to visually engage audiences and show products in action.

3. **Infographics and Visual Content:**

o **Example:** A travel agency creates engaging infographics about popular destinations, offering travel tips and interesting facts. These infographics are shared on social media to drive engagement and reach.

4. **Podcasts and Interviews:**

o **Example:** A consulting company launches a podcast where it interviews thought leaders and industry experts. This allows you to share valuable insights while increasing brand visibility.

5. **Case Studies and Customer Testimonials:**

o **Example:** A software company posts detailed case studies and testimonials from satisfied customers on its website, demonstrating the effectiveness of its products and building trust with prospects.

6. **E-books and Guides:**

o **Example:** A fitness company offers free nutrition and workout e-books in exchange for visitors' email addresses, fueling its email marketing strategy.

7. **Interactive Content:**

- Example: A personal finance site creates interactive calculators and quizzes to help users manage their budget and investments, increasing engagement and time spent on the site.

8. **Guest Blogging Articles:**
- Example: A marketing consultant writes guest posts for popular industry blogs, sharing his expertise and driving traffic to his personal website.

9. **Personalized Newsletters:**
- Example: An online store sends personalized newsletters with product recommendations based on customer preferences and purchasing history.

10. **Seasonal and Thematic Content:**
- Example: A clothing brand creates and shares content themed around holidays and seasons, like summer style guides or holiday gift ideas.

By implementing these content strategies, businesses can not only attract and retain the attention of their target audience, but also strengthen their market positioning and improve their online performance.

Future Trends and Forecasts

Evolution of Digital Marketing

1. **Introduction :**

o   Digital marketing has undergone rapid evolution over the past few decades, influenced by technological advances, changes in consumer behaviors and the emergence of new communication channels. This section explores current trends and forecasts the future of digital marketing.

2. Integration of Artificial Intelligence:

o   AI is transforming digital marketing by enabling deeper personalization, predictive analysis of consumer trends, and automation of marketing tasks. Chatbots, personalized recommendations and real-time campaign optimization are examples of the application of AI.

3. Increased Data Usage:

o   Data plays a central role in modern digital marketing. Big data analytics allows businesses to better understand their customers and optimize their marketing strategies for more effective results.

4. Omnichannel Marketing:

o   The omnichannel approach, which delivers a consistent customer experience across multiple platforms and touchpoints, is becoming the norm. This strategy enables seamless interaction with customers, whether online, on mobile or in-store.

5. Augmented Reality and Virtual Reality:

o   AR and VR offer immersive and interactive experiences, opening new avenues for digital marketing. Brands can use these technologies for virtual product trials, immersive brand experiences, and interactive advertisements.

6. Video Marketing and Live Streaming:

o   Video content continues to dominate, with a rise in the popularity of live streaming. Videos offer an engaging way to tell brand stories and connect with audiences on a more personal basis.

7. Growing Importance of Voice SEO:

o   With the growing popularity of voice assistants, voice SEO is becoming crucial. Optimizing content for voice search requires a different approach, focusing on more conversational phrases and direct questions.

8. Data Confidentiality and Regulations:

o   Growing concerns around data privacy and regulations such as GDPR are influencing digital marketing. Companies must be transparent in the collection and use of data while respecting user privacy.

9. Evolution of Social Networks:

o   Social media platforms are constantly evolving, with new features and algorithms. Brands must adapt quickly to these changes to maintain engagement and reach.

10. **Conclusion :**

o   The future of digital marketing will be characterized by further integration of advanced technologies, a focus on personalized user experience, and continued adaptation to the rapid changes in the digital landscape. Businesses that embrace these developments will be better positioned to succeed in an increasingly digitalized environment.

Future of Electronic Commerce

1. **Introduction :**

o   E-commerce is constantly evolving, driven by technological innovations, changes in consumer habits and growing customer expectations. This section explores emerging trends and predictions for the future of e-commerce.

2. **Advanced Customization:**

o   Personalization will become even more sophisticated through the use of artificial intelligence and machine learning. E-commerce sites will be able to offer tailored shopping experiences, recommending products based on individual preferences, purchase history and browsing behavior.

3. Integration of Augmented Reality:

o Augmented reality (AR) will transform the online shopping experience by allowing customers to view products in their own environment before making a purchase. This will help reduce uncertainty and increase customer satisfaction.

4. Voice Commerce and Smart Assistants:

o With the growing popularity of voice assistants, voice commerce will become an important avenue for online shopping. Consumers will be able to make purchases simply by using their voice, making the shopping experience more convenient and accessible.

5. Simplified and Secure Payments:

o Payment technologies will evolve to provide faster, safer and more convenient transactions. Contactless payments, digital wallets and cryptocurrencies will grow in popularity, giving consumers more options and better security.

6. Innovative Logistics and Delivery:

o Advances in logistics and delivery, such as drones and autonomous vehicles, will revolutionize the way products are delivered. Same-day or even within-hour delivery could become the norm for many online retailers.

7. **Sustainability and Ethical Trade:**

o   Sustainability will become a crucial aspect of e-commerce. Consumers expect ethical and eco-friendly business practices, which will push companies to adopt sustainable packaging, transparent supply chains and eco-friendly products.

8. **Omnichannel Experience:**

o   The omnichannel shopping experience, providing a consistent customer experience across multiple channels (online, mobile, in-store), will become essential. Technologies like beacons and interactive in-store displays will further integrate online experiences

o   and offline.

9. **Data Analysis and Decision Making:**

o   Data analytics will play an even bigger role in e-commerce. Insights from data will help businesses make informed decisions, optimize operations and improve customer experiences.

10. **Conclusion :**

o   The future of e-commerce will be marked by continued innovation, increased personalization, advanced technology integration and a growing commitment to sustainability. Businesses that quickly adapt to these changes will be better positioned to succeed in a rapidly changing market.

Developments in Artificial Intelligence

1. Introduction :

o   Artificial intelligence (AI) is redefining many industries, including marketing, e-commerce, manufacturing and services. This section explores recent developments in AI and their potential impact on various industries.

2. Process Automation and Optimization:

o   AI enables the automation of repetitive tasks and the optimization of business processes. In the future, we can expect to see AI systems supporting complex functions, improving efficiency and reducing operational costs.

3. Personalization of Marketing and Advertising:

o   AI technologies are increasingly being used to personalize marketing and advertising experiences. They help analyze consumer data in real time and adjust advertising messages to target individual preferences, improving engagement and campaign effectiveness.

4. Forecasts and Predictive Analysis:

o   AI plays a crucial role in predictive analytics, helping businesses anticipate market trends, consumer behaviors and

potential risks. This ability to predict
helps businesses make proactive and
strategic decisions.

5. **Improved Customer Experience:**

o   AI is used to improve customer
experience through intelligent chatbots,
virtual assistants and personalized
recommendations. These technologies
provide fast and personalized customer
service, increasing customer satisfaction
and loyalty.

6. **Developments in Machine Learning:**

o   Machine learning, a branch of AI,
continues to evolve, allowing machines to
learn and adapt without being explicitly
programmed. This opens possibilities for
more intuitive and intelligent applications
in various fields.

7. **Impact on Decision Making:**

o   AI provides deep insights and data
analysis that helps leaders make more
informed decisions. In the future, AI could
play a greater role in strategic decision-
making within organizations.

8. **Security and Confidentiality:**

o   With the increase in the use of
AI, issues of data security and privacy
become paramount. Future developments
in AI will need to address these concerns,
ensuring data protection and regulatory

compliance.

9. **Intersectoral Integration:**

○ AI is finding applications in a growing range of sectors, from healthcare to finance, education and transportation. This cross-sector integration of AI will drive innovation and the creation of new business opportunities.

10. **Conclusion :**

○ Developments in AI promise to radically transform the landscape of business and society. Companies that embrace and integrate these technologies will be better equipped to face future challenges and seize new opportunities in a world increasingly driven by data and artificial intelligence.

Trends in Social Media

1. **Introduction :**

○ Social media continues to evolve at a rapid pace, significantly influencing the way brands interact with their audiences. This section explores current and future social media trends and their impact on marketing and communications.

2. **Increased Video Engagement:**

○ Videos, especially short formats and stories, are gaining popularity on social platforms. Brands are increasingly using video content to engage their audiences in creative and dynamic ways.

3. Rise of Micro-Influencers:

o   Micro-influencers, with their smaller but highly engaged audiences, are becoming a preferred choice for brands. They offer higher authenticity and level of trust compared to influencers with large audiences.

4. Social Commerce and Integrated Purchasing:

o   Social media platforms are increasingly integrating e-commerce features, allowing users to purchase products directly through posts and stories. This trend is transforming the way consumers discover and purchase products.

5. Use of Augmented Reality:

o   Augmented reality (AR) on social media, particularly through filters and interactive experiences, offers new opportunities for brands to create immersive and memorable experiences for users.

6. Increased Importance of Authenticity:

o   Consumers are looking for authenticity in the brands they follow on social media. Content that reflects real stories, brand values and increased transparency is gaining popularity.

7. **Engagement through User Generated Content:**

o   User-generated content (UGC) continues to be a powerful tool for brands on social media. Encouraging customers to share their own content builds engagement and trust.

8. **Focus on Social Responsibility:**

o   Brands use social media to highlight their commitment to social and environmental causes. This trend reflects a growing awareness of corporate social responsibilities.

9. **Evolution of Algorithms:**

o   Constant changes in social platform algorithms require brands to adapt quickly to maintain visibility and engagement. Understanding and adapting to these algorithms is crucial for success.

10. **Integration of Chatbots and AI:**

o   Integrating chatbots and artificial intelligence for customer service and personalized engagement is becoming more common. These technologies enable rapid and personalized interaction on a large scale.

11. **Conclusion :**

o   Current trends in social media indicate a shift towards more interactivity, authenticity and technological integration. Brands that adapt to these trends and incorporate them into their social media strategies will be better positioned to engage their audiences and build their online presence.

Future of Programmatic Advertising

1. **Introduction :**
- Programmatic advertising, which uses algorithms and automated technologies to buy and sell advertising space, is transforming the digital advertising landscape. This section explores future trends and expected developments in this area.

2. **Increased Integration of AI and Machine Learning:**
- Artificial intelligence (AI) and machine learning will play an increasingly central role in programmatic advertising. These technologies will enable more precise optimization of campaigns, better targeting of audiences and real-time analysis of advertising performance.

3. **Omnichannel Advertising:**
- Programmatic advertising will expand beyond traditional digital platforms to include connected TV, digital billboards and other channels. This omnichannel approach will provide advertisers with

broader reach and increased consistency in their advertising campaigns.

4. Data Transparency and Confidentiality:

o   With concerns about data privacy increasing, transparency will become a crucial aspect of programmatic advertising. Advertisers and platforms will need to ensure the protection of user data while maintaining transparency in targeting and measurement processes.

5. Increased Automation and Efficiency:

o   Automation in programmatic advertising will improve, allowing advertisers to launch and manage campaigns more efficiently. This includes automating content creation, ad space buying, and campaign optimization.

6. Large-Scale Customization:

o   The ability to personalize advertising messages on a large scale will be strengthened. Advertisers will be able to create highly personalized ads that resonate with specific audience segments, improving engagement and relevance.

7. Impact of 5G and New Technologies:

o   The arrival of 5G and other advanced technologies will open up new possibilities for programmatic advertising, particularly in terms of ad loading speed, ad format quality and interactive experiences.

8. **Evolution of Advertising Formats:**

o   Advertising formats will continue to evolve, with an increase in immersive and interactive ads, such as augmented reality and virtual reality, providing more engaging experiences for users.

9. **Regulatory   Challenges   and Opportunities:**

o   Changes in regulation, such as data privacy laws, will present both challenges and opportunities for programmatic advertising. Market players will need to adapt to these changes while exploiting new opportunities to innovate.

10. **Conclusion:**

o   The future of programmatic advertising is bright, with technological advancements that will continue to transform the way ads are targeted, delivered and measured. Businesses that embrace these changes and adapt quickly will be better positioned to take advantage of the opportunities presented by this rapid evolution in the advertising market.

Innovations in UX/UI Design

1. **Introduction:**

o   UX/UI design is an ever-evolving field, shaped by technological advancements and changes in user behaviors. This section explores current and future innovations in UX/UI design and their impact on the creation of digital products.

2. **User-Centered Design:**

o   The user-centered approach will remain at the heart of UX/UI design. Designers will continue to create intuitive interfaces and user experiences based on a deep understanding of user needs, wants and behaviors.

3. **Integration of AI and Machine Learning:**

o   Artificial intelligence and machine learning will transform UX/UI design by enabling more intelligent and adaptive interfaces. These technologies will enable the creation of personalized experiences in real time, based on user interactions and preferences.

4. **Design for Foldable and Flexible Screens:**

o   With the emergence of foldable and flexible screens, UX/UI designers will need to innovate to create fluid and consistent experiences on these new formats. This includes designing interfaces that dynamically adapt to different screen configurations.

5. **Augmented Reality and Virtual Reality:**

o   AR and VR will provide new

opportunities for UX/UI design. Designers will explore ways to create immersive and interactive experiences, integrating real-world elements with enriched digital information.

6. **Voice Design and Conversational Interfaces:**

o The design of voice and conversational interfaces will increase in importance. UX/UI designers will work on user experiences where voice and natural dialogue play a central role, particularly in applications for voice assistants and chatbots.

7. **Accessibility and Inclusivity:**

o Accessibility and inclusiveness will remain essential aspects of UX/UI design. Designers will strive to create digital products that are accessible to everyone, taking into account the diverse abilities and needs of users.

8. **Micro-interactions and Animations:**

o Micro-interactions and sophisticated animations will continue to enrich the user experience. These subtle but powerful elements improve engagement and help guide users through interfaces in an intuitive way.

9. **Ethical and Responsible Design:**

o Ethical and responsible design

will become an increasingly important subject. UX/UI designers will take into account the social and environmental impact of their creations, ensuring that they promote responsible and sustainable practices.

10. **Conclusion :**

o   Innovations in UX/UI design will play a crucial role in defining the future of digital products. By staying at the forefront of technology trends and focusing on user needs, UX/UI designers will continue to create memorable and meaningful experiences that shape our daily interaction with technology.

Sustainable Development and Corporate Responsibility

1. **Introduction :**

o   Sustainability and corporate responsibility have become essential elements in modern business strategy. This section explores how businesses are integrating sustainable practices into their operations and their impact on society and the environment.

2. **Integration of Sustainable Development into Commercial Operations:**

o   Companies are adopting sustainable

practices in their operations, such as using renewable resources, reducing waste, and improving energy efficiency. These practices are not only beneficial to the environment, but they can also lead to long-term cost savings.

3. **Corporate Social Responsibility (CSR):**

o CSR is becoming a crucial aspect of corporate reputation. Initiatives such as supporting local communities, employee wellness programs, and contributions to social causes strengthen the company's position as a responsible actor in society.

4. **Transparency and Sustainability Reporting:**

o Transparency in sustainability practices is increasingly demanded by consumers and stakeholders. Companies publish detailed sustainability reports to show their commitment to responsible business practices.

5. **Circular Economy and Sustainable Business Models:**

o The circular economy, which aims to minimize waste and maximize the use of resources, is growing in popularity. Companies are adopting sustainable business models that incorporate the reuse, recycling and regeneration of products and materials.

6. Sustainable Innovation:

○ Innovation in sustainable products and services is a growing area. Companies invest in research and development to create solutions that address environmental challenges while meeting consumer needs.

7. Stakeholder Engagement:

○ Companies actively engage stakeholders, including customers, employees, suppliers and local communities, in their sustainability initiatives. This collaborative approach strengthens accountability and impact of sustainability efforts.

8. Impact on the Supply Chain:

○ Sustainability in the supply chain is essential. Companies work with their suppliers to ensure ethical and sustainable practices from production to distribution.

9. Challenges and Opportunities:

○ Although integrating sustainability presents challenges, such as higher upfront costs and the need to change established processes, it also offers significant opportunities in terms of innovation, market differentiation and regulatory compliance.

10. Conclusion :

○ Sustainability and corporate

responsibility will continue to be key factors in business success. By adopting sustainable practices, businesses can not only contribute positively to society and the environment, but also strengthen their position and competitiveness in the market.

Evolution of Influencer Marketing

1. **Introduction :**
o   Influencer marketing, which involves working with influential individuals to promote products or services, has grown rapidly. This section examines the past evolution and future trends of influencer marketing.

2. **Diversification of Platforms:**
o   While platforms like Instagram and YouTube remain popular for influencer marketing, other emerging platforms, such as TikTok and Twitch, are growing in importance. Brands are looking to leverage these new channels to reach diverse audiences.

3. **Increase in Micro-Influencers:**
o   Micro-influencers, with their smaller but highly engaged audiences, are becoming increasingly popular with brands. Their authenticity and proximity to their audience often provides better

engagement and higher ROI.

4. Performance measurement and ROI:

o   The focus is on accurately measuring performance and return on investment in influencer marketing. Brands use advanced tools and technologies to track the engagement, reach and impact of influencer campaigns.

5. Quality and Authenticity Content:

o   Authenticity remains a key element to success in influencer marketing. Consumers are looking for authentic, quality content rather than obvious promotional messages. Influencers are therefore encouraged to create content that truly reflects their own voices and styles.

6. Long-Term Relationships:

o   Brands are moving towards long-term partnerships with influencers, rather than one-off collaborations. These lasting relationships help build brand consistency and increased audience loyalty.

7. Integration of Augmented Reality:

o   The use of augmented reality in influencer marketing is on the rise, providing immersive and interactive experiences. Influencers can use AR to showcase products in a more engaging way.

8. **Ethics and Transparency:**

o   Questions of ethics and transparency become crucial. Influencers and brands are increasingly required to clearly disclose paid partnerships and adhere to advertising guidelines.

9. **Virtual and AI Influencers:**

o   The emergence of virtual influencers, created by artificial intelligence, represents a new frontier in influencer marketing. These digital personas can provide unique brand control and constant availability.

10. **Conclusion :**

o   The future of influencer marketing will be characterized by greater diversification of platforms, a focus on authenticity and quality of content, and the use of advanced technologies for measurement and engagement. Brands that adapt to these developments will continue to benefit from the powerful impact of influencer marketing.

Emerging Technologies

1. **Introduction :**

o   Emerging technologies are actively shaping the future of various sectors, providing new opportunities and challenges. This section explores key emerging technologies and their potential impact on business, society and the environment.

2. **Artificial Intelligence and Machine Learning:**

o AI and machine learning continue to advance, providing capabilities for advanced data analysis, process automation and service personalization. These technologies are transforming industries such as healthcare, finance, marketing and manufacturing.

3. **Blockchain and Cryptocurrencies:**

o Blockchain, beyond cryptocurrencies, offers promising applications in terms of data security, transaction transparency and decentralization. It has the potential to revolutionize areas like supply chain, electronic voting and copyright management.

4. **Internet of Things (IoT):**

o IoT connects everyday devices to the Internet, enabling data collection and exchange. This increased connectivity opens possibilities in smart home and city management, precision agriculture, and predictive maintenance in industry.

5. **Augmented Reality and Virtual Reality:**

o AR and VR deliver immersive

experiences, changing the way consumers interact with products and brands. They find applications in education, entertainment, retail and real estate.

6. **Autonomous Vehicles and Drones:**

o   Advances in autonomous vehicles and drones promise to transform transportation and logistics. These technologies could reduce road accidents, optimize the delivery of goods and revolutionize personal transportation.

7. **3D Printing and Additive Manufacturing:**

o   3D printing continues to evolve, enabling rapid, custom production of parts and products. It has a significant impact in areas such as manufacturing, medicine (prosthetics, implants) and construction.

8. **Renewable Energy and Green Technologies:**

o   Innovations in renewable energy and green technologies are essential to meeting the challenges of climate change. They include the development of new energy sources, sustainable materials and eco-responsible production practices.

9. **Biotechnology and Personalized Medicine:**

o   Advances in biotechnology and personalized medicine offer promising prospects for the treatment of complex diseases and personalization of healthcare, based on individual genetics.

10. **Cybersecurity and Data Protection:**

o   With the increase in connectivity and data generated, cybersecurity is becoming a major issue. Emerging technologies in this area aim to protect sensitive information and prevent cyberattacks.

11. **Conclusion :**

o   Emerging technologies represent immense potential to transform industries and improve quality of life. However, they also raise ethical, regulatory and safety issues that need to be addressed. Businesses and corporations that adapt and integrate these technologies responsibly and innovatively will be better prepared for the future.

Consumer Behavior Forecasts

1. **Introduction :**

o   Understanding and anticipating consumer behavior is crucial for businesses wanting to stay competitive. This section explores predictions about the evolution of consumer behaviors, influenced by technological, social and economic changes.

2. **Increase in Ecological Awareness:**

o   Consumers are increasingly aware of environmental issues. Growing demand for sustainable, ethical and eco-friendly products is expected. Companies will therefore have to integrate sustainable practices into their offerings to meet these expectations.

3. **Preference for Personalized Experiences:**

o   Personalization is becoming a key factor in purchasing decisions. Consumers expect tailored experiences, whether in e-commerce, marketing or customer service. Businesses will need to use data and AI to deliver personalized experiences.

4. **Increased Use of Digital Technologies:**

o   With increasing digitalization, consumers will continue to adopt and adapt to new technologies. This includes the increased use of e-commerce platforms, mobile applications, and voice assistants for purchases.

5. **Search for Authenticity and Transparency:**

o   Consumers value authenticity and transparency in brands. They are increasingly likely to research information about products and companies before making purchasing decisions and prefer brands that are honest and open.

6. Sensitivity to Social Issues:

o   Social issues, such as equality, diversity and inclusion, are increasingly influencing consumer choices. Businesses will need to show their commitment to these issues to maintain a strong connection with their audience.

7. Preference for Online Shopping:

o   The trend toward online shopping, accelerated by the COVID-19 pandemic, is expected to continue. Consumers value the convenience, variety, and often the best prices available online.

8. Request for Fast and Efficient Services:

o   Consumers expect fast and efficient services. Speedy delivery, ease of returns and responsive customer service will be key factors in winning and retaining customers.

9. Evolution of Payment Methods:

o   Payment methods will continue to evolve, with increased adoption of contactless payments, digital wallets and perhaps cryptocurrencies, providing greater convenience and security.

10. Conclusion :

o   Companies must remain attentive to these changes in consumer behavior to adapt their strategies accordingly. Understanding and meeting evolving consumer expectations will be essential to delivering relevant and engaging experiences, and maintaining a competitive advantage in an ever-changing marketplace.

Digital Marketing FAQs

1. **What is digital marketing?**
   - Answer: Digital marketing encompasses all marketing activities that use digital channels to promote products or services. This includes SEO, content marketing, social media, email marketing, online advertising, and more.
2. **How can SEO benefit my business?**
   - Answer: SEO (Search Engine Optimization) helps improve the visibility of your website on search engines. This can lead to increased organic traffic, better brand credibility, and ultimately increased sales and conversions.
3. **How important is social media in digital marketing?**
   - Answer: Social media allows businesses to reach and engage a large audience. They offer unique opportunities for brand building, targeted advertising, customer engagement and obtaining

direct consumer feedback.

4. **What is the difference between inbound and outbound marketing?**

o Answer: Inbound marketing focuses on creating quality content to attract customers to your business, while outbound marketing involves more direct approaches, like advertisements and cold calling, to obtain sales.

5. **How to measure the effectiveness of a digital marketing campaign?**

o Answer: Effectiveness can be measured using various metrics, such as website traffic, conversion rate, social media engagement, ROI (return on investment), and other KPIs (key performance indicators).

6. **What is content marketing?**

o Answer: Content marketing involves creating and sharing informative and relevant materials (like blogs, videos, infographics) to attract and retain a target audience, and ultimately, to drive customer action.

7. **What are the advantages of paid online advertising?**

o Answer: Paid online advertising, like Pay-Per-Click (PPC) ads, provides immediate visibility, precise audience targeting, and the ability to directly measure the effectiveness of your ads.

8. **How has digital marketing evolved with mobile technology?**

o   Answer: With the increase in smartphone usage, mobile marketing has become crucial. This includes website optimization for mobile, mobile apps, SMS marketing, and mobile-friendly content strategies.

9. **What is marketing automation and how can it help my business?**

o   Answer: Marketing automation uses software to automate repetitive marketing tasks. This can improve efficiency, reduce human errors and enable personalized communication at scale.

10. **How to integrate sustainable development into digital marketing?**

o   Answer: Integrating sustainability involves promoting ethical and environmentally friendly practices in your marketing strategies, communicating your sustainability efforts, and adopting business practices that support social and environmental responsibility.

THANKS

In writing this book, I have had the privilege of drawing on the knowledge, experience, and support of many exceptional people. It is important for me to take a moment to express my gratitude to everyone who contributed to the completion of this work.

First of all, I would like to thank my colleagues and mentors in the field of digital marketing. Your expertise, insights and advice have been an invaluable source of inspiration throughout this project. Your contributions to the world of digital marketing continue to shape the industry, and your influence is reflected in the pages of this book.

Special thanks to the editorial team and reviewers for their hard work, attention to detail, and commitment to maintaining the highest quality. Your professionalism and dedication have greatly improved this manuscript, and I am deeply grateful for your support throughout this process.

I would also like to express my gratitude to my family and friends for their unwavering support, encouragement and patience. Your understanding and support during the long hours spent writing and researching have been a pillar of my motivation and perseverance.

A special thanks to the digital marketing community – practitioners, academics, students and enthusiasts – for their relentless curiosity and thirst for learning. Your commitment to excellence and innovation continues to inspire my work and thinking.

Finally, I would like to thank each reader who chose to delve into this book. Your interest in digital marketing and your desire to develop professionally are the reason for this book. I hope you find in these pages valuable information, inspiring ideas, and practical strategies for navigating the dynamic world of digital marketing.

Kind regards,
Vincent Lefebvre

From the same author :

available on Amazon.fr

Vegan Kids: A practical book for families who want to adopt a healthy and sustainable vegan diet

Urban Garden: The Essential Guide to Creating Eco-responsible and Inclusive Green Spaces

Resilience Handbook: Discover how to transform societal conflicts into growth opportunities

What is leadership in 2024?: Adapting to today's changes and challenges to thrive tomorrow

How to get out of your burnout in 2024?: Find your path to healing and rediscover the joy of living

VINCENT LEFEBVRE

SORTIR DE SON BURNOUT EN 2024 ?

Trouvez votre chemin vers la guérison et redécouvrez la joie de vivre

Ron Goldsmith
EDITIONS

What is happiness in 2024?: The reference book for feeling good in your body and in your skin this year and beyond

VINCENT LEFEBVRE

C'EST QUOI LE BONHEUR EN 2024 ?

le livre référence pour se sentir bien dans son corps et dans sa peau cette année et les suivantes

Ron Goldsmith
EDITIONS

What is success in 2024?: Examining yesterday's successes to anticipate tomorrow's opportunities

VINCENT LEFEBVRE

C'EST QUOI LE SUCCES EN 2024 ?

Examiner les succès d'hier pour anticiper les opportunités de demain

Ron Goldsmith
EDITIONS

What is parenthood in 2024?: Practical solutions for successful parenting in the digital age

What is sustainable
development in 2024?: The
book that gives you the tools
to change the world and puts
sustainable development
within everyone's reach

What is Freemasonry in 2024?: Discover how Freemasonry adapts to the challenges of the 21st century and contributes to the improvement of society

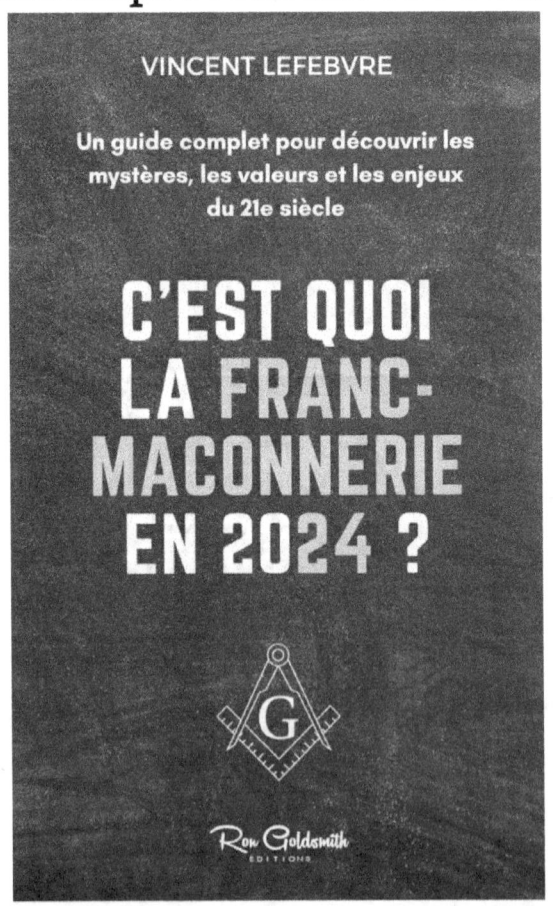

Freemasonry and AI: From the lodge to the algorithm, embark on an exploration of AI with a Masonic compass

Giftedness and Creativity: Journey to the heart of emotional intelligence, the key to understanding gifted people